Pieman

The Papa D Story

June V. Bourgo
Dennis Bourgo

Copyright (C) 2022 June V. Bourgo, Dennis Bourgo

Layout design and Copyright (C) 2022 by Next Chapter

Published 2022 by Next Chapter

Edited by Graham (Fading Street Services)

Mass Market Paperback Edition

All rights reserved. No part of this book may be reproduced or transmitted in any form or by any means, electronic or mechanical, including photocopying, recording, or by any information storage and retrieval system, without the author's permission.

...to Lily Legge Wood
Thank you, Nana, for teaching me to love cooking!

Acknowledgments

When the story is a partial biography about a specific time in my life, it's easy to pay tribute to those who contributed to the success of my small enterprise in those five years on the British Columbia coast and the few years which followed in the interior. I deliberately left out the names of those mentioned in the book out of respect for their privacy unless permission was given.

First and foremost, I thank my wife, June, for not only supporting my endeavours but for her unwavering belief in my business and personal aspirations. She played an integral part in the success of my accomplishments, not only during the time written about in this story but throughout our thirty-seven years together. As my partner, and a successful woman in her own right, my respect for her intelligence and talents is immense. Her contribution to the writing of this book and the vast experience she brought to it is so appreciated.

A big thank you to the business investors—you know who you are, and you were my angels. A shout out to the original landowner and his family, to the contractors who helped me achieve my vision, the ladies who rented space in my kitchen, and everyone who worked with me.

And of course, the business would have been nothing without the patrons, many of whom became friends. Your support, enthusiasm, and humour contributed to the magical success of the little pie shop.

A special thank you to my editor, Charlee Redman Bezilla, for her invaluable edits and input.

To my beta readers, Megan Herlaar, Sandra J. Jackson, and Ron Bagliere, thank you for your support and validation.

And, of course, to Miika and the team at Next Chapter Publishing for bringing this story to life.

But the success I achieved came from so many people and events in my life even before starting this project. Everything I'd questioned and hopefully learned previously, from the positive influences of others and lessons from the negative ones, and the hundreds of eclectic books I'd read over the years—all contributed to the mindset I'd reached and developed as I began this endeavour.

I thank my Nana for her stories about the ranch on the Old Man River in Fort MacLeod, Alberta and for teaching me to cook, and my Grampa for sharing his life-long wisdom in his easy, laid-back style.

And last, but not least, a big thank-you to my children and grandchildren who have no idea of the impact they've made in my life. My hope is this snippet into my world helps them understand a little more about their crazy Papa and know they are all loved.

Thank you one and all.

Preface

For most of my adult life, my work centred on running self-owned businesses. My love of cooking and artistic talent, nurtured by our family doctor who enrolled me in art classes at the age of six, played a large part in my business life. Over the years, I've managed and owned restaurants and graphic arts and signage companies.

And through my lifelong love and study of science and quantum physics, developed a solar-powered water pump that was way ahead of its time when solar power was in its infancy and cost a fortune to use. During the nineteen-eighties close friends in Victoria who were working on scientific research projects, asked me to bring my pump onboard under my own company. These were my days of chasing big money. My company was under contract with a parent company, funded by federal government scientific research monies. My lofty idea of developing a solar-powered water pump for third-world countries without electrical power for water systems was halted when we hit a wall on how to store battery power from a solar source to keep the system working. This dilemma took me to Paris, France as a guest of Aerospatiale, a state-owned aerospace manufacturer that built both civilian and mil-

Preface

itary aircraft. They had developed a short-term energy storage device (MAG-LEV) for emergency purposes to protect communications that were buried under the city and around the country. I was there to see if it was possible to downsize their system to work with my project. They were very excited about working with us. But on my return home, the parent company lost its funding. The government had cut back funding for scientific research and invited me to apply for other funds and grants. I spent months chasing the dream and made it to second place with my research accreditation for an almost million-dollar grant—but lost out. With my funding gone, I had no choice but to close down and move on. It was a hard pill to swallow. That year I had a tax bill of three million dollars owed to Revenue. The good that came out of that project was once the paperwork was audited and my project accreditation was presented to Revenue, I received a substantial tax refund and tax credits which voided my hefty tax bill. It was a funding project with a lot of flaws but in the end, I benefited. We bought a house on the Sunshine Coast where this book takes place. I tell you this as an explanation of where I had been and where I ended up. And why becoming the Pieman was such an important experience and growth period in my life that had nothing to do with chasing or achieving money.

I chose to write this book because June and I, in our thirty-seven years together, have discovered there's a kind of 'magic' at work sometimes and if you allow yourself to believe, to trust your intuition or 'gut', you won't miss out. The things that came about in this period of our lives were magical. So, open your mind and allow that things can go 'right' sometimes.

This story covers a period towards the end of my working life which I discovered to be the most fulfilling yet.

Preface

Read on...

> Dennis Bourgo aka Papa D

Preface

The biography in this book is reflective of my husband's journey to self. As his long-time partner in life, of course, I'm a part of his story. The birth and writing of this project were solely his and he spent many months putting it down on paper. My role, as a fiction writer, was to take his words and craft them into a creative non-fiction piece of work; a challenge and a refreshing change in my writing life.

Working together was another challenge, and, surprisingly, we rose to the occasion. Our many talks about this period of our lives allowed me to add memories he'd forgotten and brought forth some we'd both left behind. We were reminded of the struggles we'd shared and conquered in our life journey together. And despite a few 'harshly worded' editorial arguments, I believe the telling of this story has brought us closer.

June V. Bourgo

Chapter 1

In the Beginning...

It was 1988 and I was working a part-time gig at a Legion, nicknamed 'the little legion that could' in a rural area of the Sunshine Coast, known as Roberts Creek. It's a heavily treed part of the lower coast on the Pacific Ocean. A peninsula, accessible only by ferry boat due to the Coastal Mountain Range of beautiful British Columbia. The Sunshine Coast lies north of the lower mainland of the west coast, which includes the city of Vancouver and its metropolitan cities and townships. We'd recently purchased a home in Roberts Creek, known as 'Gumboot Nation', gumboots being a staple for life during the spring rains.

We were enjoying our new country living on the Sunshine Coast with two teens, cats, dogs, horses, and chickens. A more laid-back style of living compared to the city. While it was a beautiful experience, reality set in pretty fast. We had to make a living. In those days, work was limited on the coast, and anyone who asked how residents made a living was told they cut firewood and sold it to each other. My wife, June, kept her secure job at a telecommunications company in Vancouver and commuted by ferry five days a week, along with many other coasters who worked in the city. Friday night commutes on the boat back to our little paradise resembled a party-like atmosphere for the commuters. Smoking wasn't permitted inside, so they'd head up to the open-top deck. The staff gave the smokers a blind eye if some were into wacky tobaccy, and others had a beer can or two in a cup holder hiding the label. One Friday evening, halfway home, one of the crew members who worked up on the bridge approached a group standing on the top deck. He said, "Hey guys, the captain sent me to ask if you would all mind moving down the boat." He pointed to something above their heads. "That's our air vent into the bridge, we're all getting stoned." (We Canadians are so polite.)

I'd picked up a risky job of catering at another Legion 'up coast' in Madeira Park, but soon the local 'little legion that could' offered me a Saturday night gig barbequing steaks, on the back deck beside a fast-running, picturesque creek. The offer came one Saturday night when my wife and I decided to go for a steak dinner at our local legion. When we arrived, the current chef was arguing with a customer on the deck that had brought his steak back three times, insisting it wasn't cooked enough. The customer wanted it more than well-done, and the frustrated chef had reached his boiling point. To our shock, and the customers, the chef skewered his steak with a fork and yelled, "You want well-done, well, here's well done." He chucked the steak through the air and last we saw, it floated off down the creek in the fast-moving water and disappeared.

He turned to me and said, "Dennis, you're a cook, take over—I quit." He went inside, ordered a pint, and sat with the customers waiting for their dinners. The legion executives were aghast and rushed outside where I was burning a steak to appease the upset customer. They offered me the gig on the spot.

Thus, began my weekend contract: Saturday night barbeque of eight-ounce New York strip steak, baked potato, garden salad, and garlic bread; Friday night roast beef (two roasts, one well-done for the English members, one medium rare for the rest), Yorkshire pudding, mashed potatoes, carrots, peas, and gravy. All this for six dollars a plate. A successful venture that brought in anywhere from fifty to a hundred folks and became a hit. Soon people from all over the coast were coming and I had a 'following'. My down-home style of cooking meshed well with the down-to-earth nature of my rural customers. As for the English member who wanted his steak well-done; it took me three Saturdays to figure it out. The first time, he said, 'almost, but not quite'. Second time, 'close'. Third time 'perfect'. The secret to his steak was to put it on the barbie thirty minutes before we opened for business. By the time he and his wife arrived, it was almost ready, leaving him time for a drink before dinner. When presented with his dried-out, burnt piece of shoe leather, he was thrilled and said, "You got it!"

My appreciative customers were very generous, and upon finishing their meals, one or two would buy me a pint and place it on the deck railing where I worked. At one point, I turned to find the pints lined up down the railing. Now don't get me wrong—over the years, I've enjoyed my pints along with the best of them. But not when I'm working. I'd send them back to the 'round' table where the patrons solved the problems of the world.

During the week, I had access to the kitchen and Legion for private catering events. The Legion supplied the food for the Friday and Saturday night gigs, so I was paid a set fee under my contract, and they got the proceeds from the dinners and the bar. But I purchased the foods for the private catering gigs, so proceeds from the catering contracts were mine and the Legion kept the proceeds from the bar. It was a win-win for us both.

The only foods available to Legion members during the week were meat pies, provided by an elderly member of the Ladies Auxiliary. With the success of my catering and weekend dinners, she approached me with the news she'd decided to retire and asked if I'd like to take over providing meat pies. It was a natural progression in my business, and I agreed. She provided two types of 5-inch pies, ground beef and chicken. I asked how she made her gravies, and her reply was simple: canned mushroom soup for the beef, and canned mushroom soup for the chicken. She made her pastry with shortening and this was one of her reasons for retiring. Her hands were crippled with arthritis and making pastry had become painful.

Growing up in the Okanagan, my grandmother was a great cook. She and my grandfather were from England. They'd both come to Canada as indentured servants. Nana worked for a high-end household in Toronto for several years to pay off the cost of bringing her to Canada; Grampa worked for the Baptist Church of Canada as an indentured servant for ten years. With their debts paid off, they travelled west, met, fell in love, and married. They settled in Fort McLeod, Alberta where with other family members, they built a ranch and served in local government. But I digress. Nana's work at the ranch was to cook for the family and their workers. When the depression hit in '29, they sold the ranch and moved to British Columbia. When I was a child, she taught me how to cook, and her form of camp cooking rubbed off on me. It was her meat pie recipes that I used in my catering business. I loved to cook thanks to my Nana, and this was the start of what years later was to become 'Papa D's Comfort Foods'. As a side note, the name came from my first-born grandchildren who had two 'Papas': Papa Tom and Papa Dennis. Papa Dennis became Papa D.

Chapter 2

Full Circle...

A FEW YEARS LATER, MY WIFE AND I WERE OFFERED AN opportunity to become involved in a new enterprise. June left her job in the city, and I gave up my catering business, which I should mention was a *disastrous* decision with a bad ending. Since this is my story, I will just say be very careful about business partnerships: dissolving one can be as painful as a divorce. It was an expensive exercise—but a mistake is no longer a mistake if it becomes a lesson and ours became a life lesson well-learned. The economy on the coast was still asleep. The whole province was struggling at that time, and we found ourselves in limbo. With our children grown, we sold our property and with the profits, we said goodbye to the Sunshine Coast. We returned to the city and my wife went back to work for her previous employer. I started up a graphics business (as an artist, I had worked in graphics before and decided to return to that profession). Several years later, June was offered an early-retirement package by the company, and she accepted.

So here we were at the beginning of the millennium, two thousand A.D.—and we happily found ourselves on a beautiful, leased property, back on the Sunshine Coast. The land belonged to a nice young couple, who were now living in Vancouver. The back of the park-like hectare had once been used as a small sawmill. It consisted of a large historic barn and a cute mobile home with a clever addition, making the front room twice the size of its original design. It was set in a grove of huge cedar trees, with Gibsons Creek running along the bottom edge of the acreage.

My wife, who is six and a half years younger than me, landed a managerial job at a physiotherapy clinic. I was approaching what some people would call retirement years. Not that I intended on retiring, but I no longer had the drive to chase big money. I wanted to slow down and run a small home-based business. Remembering my previous successful years of catering on the coast, and my Nana's recipes, I decided it was time to rekindle Papa D's Comfort Foods. Namely, meat pies. Since returning to the coast, I'd been constantly baking and filling orders for my small following by using the Legion kitchen to be legal. At that time, you didn't require a business license on the Sunshine Coast if you were in the Regional District. But my dream was to build a home-based business on the property. Now this dream was stretching far beyond a lot of people's imagination.

Let me describe the property to you. First, there's a 750-foot driveway from the road to the back of the property. My friends told me no one would ever drive down a dirt driveway disappearing into a huge old-growth cedar grove looking for a meat pie. They'd be blinded by visions of Sweeney Todd.

Then, there were the leftovers from the old sawmill. Piles of sawdust, wood debris, and rusty metal machinery parts between the home and barn, including inside the old wooden structure. And there was even an old rusted-out oil tank. But as my wife always says, "Never forget the magic."

Whether I started a home-based business or not, the

property needed to be cleaned up. Two of my grandchildren lived nearby and stayed most weekends. My grandson spent many hours with me building burn piles and filling a rented dumpster, which we emptied more times than we can remember.

The historic old barn and some of its junk! The original owners of the property (which was part of a larger parcel of land at that time) were Norwegian farmers. Halfway down the bank at the back of the property leading to Gibsons Creek sits a natural pond. Above that pond, they dug a cave into the bank and built a spa. In winter, they'd build a fire and place hot rocks in the cave and sweat it out in the nude, then jump into the ice-cold pond.

As you can see in the photos, it took a lot of vision to see the possibilities.

The days were long but at the end of each day we saw progress, and once the property was cleared and the barn emptied, I began dreaming about a portable building to be converted into a commercial kitchen. The search began.

Chapter 3

Dreaming the Dream...

STARTING A HOME-BASED BUSINESS CAN BE EXHILARATING. Living where you work is great on your overhead. But choosing a food business brought many upfront costs before the doors could even be opened. First off, since our living quarters weren't big enough to build a separate commercial kitchen within the residence. We needed a separate building. And, since we only leased the acreage, building a permanent building wasn't an option. With the owner's permission, a portable building that could be moved or sold at such time as we left the property was the best option.

One day, we spotted a 'potential beauty' (definitely in the eye of the beholder). It was a forty-foot building in the style of a school portable, divided into four rooms, including a two-piece bathroom. It was perfect, and I was filled with excitement. This was my building. It was tucked away at the back of an auto wrecker's yard in town. I had some funds in my business account to get started, but in dealing with the Regional District, two expensive items were added to the list. We couldn't hook up to the residential electrical grid and were required to run a separate wire from the road (750-foot driveway, remember?), put in a new pole at the site chosen for the portable kitchen, and buy a separate meter box. And, on top of that, we had to put in a separate septic field for the kitchen because, upon inspection of the residential septic field, we were told it was too old to accommodate the house and the business. *Ouch!*

The necessity of money always rears its ugly head. Could I pull it off and get opened—or was I living on a dream and a prayer? The landowner approved the new septic field and new power pole. And why wouldn't he, since we were paying for it? He was a nice guy, but he also knew if we ever left the property, he'd have a new septic field and a new power source. It was a win-win situation for him. Plus, we'd cleaned it up for him. Our reward from him was a *very, very,* reasonable lease for both the residence and to run a business off the land. His goal wasn't to make money but to have someone on the property that looked after it.

Next, I approached the auto wrecker owner. The price he asked for the building was a fair one. Believing in the success of my business venture, but not wanting to use all my money just in the start-up phase, I asked him if he would consider payments. An honest man, known for his humour, he replied, "Yup, one payment, all cash, and I'll deliver it for free." I told him I'd get back to him. My wife, the quintessential optimist, told me to put a picture of the building on the fridge and visualize my dream. If it's meant to be it will be. I laughed because the picture below wouldn't represent the dreams of very many people—but it was mine.

Pieman

The building originally housed the radio station for the Sunshine Coast Mountain F.M., hence the bars on the windows used to protect their electronics. The school district had purchased it for use at the local high school for their broadcasting course, and now it was going to be mine (as I said, you need vision to see its potential).

While I was considering what direction to take and whether I wanted to make the final commitment to purchase the building, along came an offer of a partnership. The cynical thoughts of my past disappointments took over. *Oh, a damn partnership?* Now, this was a man I had known well for many years, even holidayed with him at one point, but still, I couldn't shake the bad taste in my mouth. He was likeable enough as a friend but as a partner? And as they say, never go into business with a friend. I had a strong memory of a conversation I'd had once with a First Nations man, successful in his own horse business. He told me, "Beware of the money man."

A bank loan was out of the question. Although we had good credit, June hadn't been at her new job long enough, and I was considered unemployed by their standards. I told the potential partner, I'd mull it over and let him know. Sometimes I've found the best 'mulling' is done over a pint or two. I went down to the Gibsons Legion for a beer and a 'mull'.

Chapter 4

The Commitment...

WHILE I WAS SITTING AND MULLING, A CASUAL acquaintance walked in with his usual group. He greeted me in his characteristic, extroverted, jovial manner, asking: "Why so glum?"

I replied I was mulling.

He left his friends and sat down with me. "What? You're usually more up than this. What's going on?" he asked.

"Since you've asked, I'm trying to set up my meat pie business on the North Road property, and I found a perfect portable building. I was set to do it on my own, as tough as it might be. Along came an offer of a partnership, which financially could be a good move and secure the business. But my gut says it's not the right move for me."

He knew of the property on North Road, as he was actively involved in purchasing properties and developments. He sat back and said, "You know me. Why didn't you come to me?"

Surprised, I said, "You're up to your ass in deals, why would you be interested in my little pie shop?"

"Sure, but Dennis, I know you, and I'm not looking for partnerships, just investments. Tell me what you need, and we'll see what I can do."

Pieman

I explained my business plan to him, and he said, "Come to my house in the morning, and I'll have some help for you."

That night I called my potential partner and declined his offer. He was pissed off—I felt relieved.

The next morning, I drove out to the investor's house, a large home sitting in a cedar forest, with an ocean view. A couple of times in past dealings, when in need of cash—an ever-present need in all small enterprises—I'd made some rash moves and regretted them. This wasn't going to be one of those times. If I didn't like the terms offered, I'd walk and struggle forward on my own—or not.

I rang the doorbell and was led to the dining room table where his wife offered me some coffee. Amid the noise of his two young, rambunctious sons, we discussed his intentions and mine.

Being a flamboyant man, he stood, shook my hand, and stated his lawyer would draw up papers formally for us to sign; meanwhile, he handed me a cheque: "You want to get started so here, take this, go get your building. And if you find yourself needing more, come back. I'll see you later."

I went straight to my bank and got the cash I needed to purchase 'my' building and drove to the auto wrecker. They agreed to do some repairs to the building and replace a couple of broken windows. I was to let them know when the lot was ready, and they'd deliver my new commercial kitchen. With a handshake (and a receipt, of course), I left, totally pumped.

It was happening.

I drove back to the property and ascertained the proper site for the building. I had to consider the water hook-up, septic field, and electrical pole location. I hired an outfit to level the site for the building placement with two loads of fill and gravel.

A week later, a sunny day dawned and down the driveway came a truck hauling a forty-foot by ten-foot building sitting at a precarious angle. I helped guide the building in place and it was levelled on wooden blocks. The truck drove off and I stood and stared, ecstatic. My building was here. Now, I had to get serious about the order of things to be done.

I contacted the regional district office, requesting a building inspector from Sechelt. He came the next day and the first requirement of my commitment hit home—the tie-down rule for portable buildings. I needed ten concrete blocks made, five for each side, and each weighing 160 pounds with a looped wire cable embedded into each one, to be hooked onto the metal frame that ran underneath the portable. A visit to a local concrete plant took care of that requirement.

Once delivered, I rented jacks and handled the grunt work of placing the new concrete blocks under the building myself, attaching the chains and turnbuckles to the metal frame.

When the building inspector returned, we sat outside and after a lengthy chat about everything other than my building; he finally asked if I'd installed the concrete blocks and turnbuckles underneath. I assured him I had and stood to show him. He smiled and said, "Oh, I'm not crawling under there."

Pieman

"What? After all my hard work, you're not even going to look at them?"

"Nah, you wouldn't have called me if it wasn't done right. I don't believe in the bylaw anyway. The reason the rule was put in place, was to keep the portable on the blocks in case of hurricane-force winds. But if that should happen, do you know what you'd have?"

"What?" I asked.

"An outdoor dance floor. The building would break off and the floor would stay intact."

Scary thought—but he issued my permit.

Chapter 5

Tradesmen woes...

It took weeks for BC Hydro to accommodate me with a new pole, run the new wire down the long driveway, and install a meter box I purchased for five hundred dollars. While that was going on the work was started to install a new septic field.

The work was first class and once it was finished the two workers presented me with a bill. They asked for cash, which was no surprise. Many contractors in those days asked for cash. It was a way of doing business back then. They did tell me that the girl in the office would mail me a receipt. Nowadays, it's hard to understand that in a rural place like the coast, a lot of work was done with cash and a handshake. Everyone trusted everyone else, and it was rare that anyone was fleeced.

Pieman

A person's word meant something in those days, and news would travel fast throughout the isolated Sunshine Coast if a wrong was done. How they handled their books wasn't my concern as long as I got a receipt for mine.

Now having said that, a few days later, a long-time friend of mine from my days in Roberts Creek visited me. He worked for the old man who owned the contracting business. He asked me if I had paid the contractors and if I'd given them cash. I told him, yes, and how much; one payment was a down payment before the work started, the other when the work was finished.

"Holy shit," he exclaimed. "I believe you Dennis, but the money never made it to the office."

The next day, he came back with the owner. Having never met the old man, he wanted to talk to me in person and get the facts for himself. He told me he believed me and that my friend had vouched for my honesty and reputation over the years. He gave me a receipt, and a few days later I heard the workmen were fired; apparently, this wasn't the first time they'd stiffed the company. And so began the first unsettling business I had to deal with regarding tradespeople.

Once Hydro finished their part of the electrical work, I hired an electrician to upgrade the wiring inside the building and connect it to the new pole. Being a former radio station, the first room you enter from outside (which we intended to use as a store) was full of outdated electronic equipment and a broadcasting booth with tons of wiring, all of which had to be ripped out. In the course of his work, the electrician discovered a leak in the ceiling. The middle of the building, being the largest room, was to be the kitchen, and the back room would be used for storage and contained a separate bathroom in one corner. Although the roof looked like it was perfectly fine, we decided to torch membrane the whole roof. Torch On roofing is made up of two layers of modified bitumen that are melted together by a torch. This creates a roof that is resistant to ultraviolet light and a waterproof barrier, ideal for the west coast's wet season. Meanwhile, the store ceiling had to be removed along with the insulation and replaced. An additional unforeseen expense.

The start of the roof repair.

Completion of the electrical work was delayed, awaiting the replacement of the ceiling and insulation. Substance abuse was a problem in this isolated rural area, and it ran rampant, especially among tradespeople. Now that's not an indictment of the people themselves. Rather, it speaks to an area suffering economically, and a lot of good, decent people falling into bad choices. It became a chore to get my electrician back to finish the work when I needed him, pushing me into a position where I had to fire him and find another electrician. Sadly, it wasn't too long after that, I heard he'd passed away from a drug overdose.

Next on the agenda was plumbing. This shouldn't

have been difficult work at all, but again my plumber held me up for weeks, finishing another job while working on mine. The bathroom, which was already complete, was easily hooked up to the new septic field and I purchased commercial-grade double sinks to be connected in the kitchen. He finished running the new pipes to the septic field, and the water supply. I thought the worst was over and began to see daylight on the horizon.

June and I got busy and began painting the outside of the building

We turned to the inside. Now that the plumbing, electrical, and roofing were finished, there wasn't a lot of structural work to do within the rooms. The walls, thermal windows, and doors were already to code; long fluorescent lights were perfect for the kitchen area, and the bathroom contained a modern toilet, sink, and fan. We set about laying commercial kitchen-grade splash-guard moulding around the bottom of the walls as required by law. We were ready for counters, two convection ovens for the kitchen, storage shelves for the storage room, and a refrigerator, freezer, and display cooler for the store.

The last thing to be completed was skirting around the outside of the building. Once again, my ever-supportive wife pitched in and after days of stooping, cut-ting, inserting, and staining we were finished. The building inspector came for one last inspection and issued our final permit.

Our last hurdle was approval from the health inspector. We failed. He decided our sinks weren't deep enough and wanted them replaced, and he told me I needed to install a grease trap under the sink. Having owned and managed restaurants in the past, I was well aware of the rules regarding grease traps. I argued the point, telling him I didn't require one because they were for kitchens that used deep fryers and dealt with a lot of fat. I used lean meats in my products and didn't require fryers. He mused on that but insisted although my volume was less than that of a restaurant kitchen, I must install one—but it could be a smaller grease trap than those in larger kitchens. *Aargh—more dollars out the door*.

We took the ferry to the mainland to visit a used commercial kitchen equipment supplier and found a small used grease trap for $280, not bad since they were about $800 new. The sinks were second-hand as well. Rebooking my plumber to make the changes, I sadly learned he'd committed suicide. My search began for another plumber. I was beginning to think my kitchen was jinxed.

Chapter 6

Seeing the Magic...

THERE WAS A SHORT WAITING PERIOD BEFORE THE NEW plumber could finish off the requested changes in the kitchen plumbing and sinks. Soon all the repairs, changes, and labour would be behind me, and I began to concentrate on what I loved best: planning my marketing, and deciding on my menu. The first thing I did was order signage for the building and the end of the driveway on the road. I installed a post with my new sign and hung two chains below it with a sign that read, 'open soon'. It was an effective teaser, with a few people driving in to see what I was all about.

One of the new companies my investor was involved with built fir decks, and they needed a show deck for their advertising. He drove in one day and asked me how I'd feel about them building a 40-foot long by 6-foot-deep deck on the front of the building as a showcase deck—for free. Guess what I said? "Hell, yeah!" It even had a wooden bar built along the edge for people who might want to sit and eat a 'hot' pie. Some magic after all.

One beautiful day, I was in the kitchen, planning my menu, and writing a shopping list for the wholesaler in Vancouver. Suddenly, a red truck sped down the driveway, hitting the brakes so hard the truck bounced sideways, and a cloud of dust filled the air. *What the hell?* I ran out of my kitchen as the dust settled, recognizing the health inspector as he stepped out of his vehicle.

"How dare you! How dare you!" he shouted.

"I have no idea what you're talking about," I said.

"Sure you do. How dare you open without final inspection and a valid health permit?"

What? "Excuse me? I'm not open. I'm still waiting for the plumber to replace the sinks and install the grease trap." I pointed to them sitting on the deck.

"You've installed a sign on the road with a red *open* hanging under it. You're open."

My thought at this point was: *And you're an idiot who can't read w*hich I wisely kept to myself. *(Well…maybe a few expletives were added in my mind as well.)*

"The sign does not say I'm open, it says 'open soon'. You can drive back up the driveway if you like and read it again."

He got in his truck and drove back down the driveway, at a slower speed I might add. I went back to the kitchen and a few minutes later, I heard him driving up the driveway. I found him on the deck, nodding, while he checked out the additional equipment yet to be installed. He put his hand out to shake mine and said, "Think we could start over?"

We shook hands and sat on the deck. "Let me tell you where I just came from," he said.

He was up at a house checking out a complaint with a man I'll leave nameless. Let's just say he's a very colourful character, well-known in the community just as much for his laid-back nature and humour when sober as for his quick, uncontrollable temper while drinking. After an altercation with him that ended badly, the health inspector found himself facing a shotgun and being ordered off the man's land. He'd left the property, just down the road from mine, physically shaking with anger and fear. When he saw my new signage, the only word that caught his attention was 'open'.

"Sorry, man. I took it out on you," he said. "You know, I just spent two years up north in Fort St. John. They live by their own rules up there. They'd do things like put their septic system uphill from their house. I was told when I transferred down here, I'd get away from the rednecks. You lot are supposed to be laid-back old hippies from the sixties and US Vietnam draft dodgers who never went home. What happened down the road this morning was a shocker."

I sat listening to his stories, letting him do the talking, bringing himself down from his bad experience. Finally, he stood. "Well, thanks for the chat." (I chuckled.) "Guess I'm off to file a report on your neighbour." As he stepped off the deck, he turned and nodded at the new sinks and grease trap. "By the way, they'll do nicely."

Not too long after, we got our health permit, and our kitchen was legal and officially open.

I stood staring at our little country kitchen, looking like it had always been there, and remembered my wife's words: *Never forget the magic!*

Chapter 7

Crusts 'n' Guts...

IT WAS TIME TO GET DOWN TO SOME SERIOUS BAKING, AND I started with my inherited basic pie recipes: beefsteak, steak and kidney, ground beef 'n' onion, chicken deluxe (chicken and veggies), and the old French Canadian tourtière (ground beef and pork mixed with mashed potatoes and a touch of allspice). My pastry was a recipe done the old English way: lard (not shortening), eggs, unbleached white flour, salt, cold water, and the defining ingredient—vinegar. Yup, that simple! The crowning glory of my pastry was the top. Once the layer was placed over the filling, I tore the pastry into uneven pieces and piled them on top, brushing it with a beaten egg. The result gave my pies a funky, golden-brown appearance that most people loved, and it became my signature that said: *This is a Papa D pie*. Customers said they had a cool, 'old English' look to them, so I stuck to my funk and that was a part of the magic. I recall one customer at the Legion who gushed about how she couldn't get enough of my crusts—and she loved 'the guts' too.

I made a lofty decision since we were living in a 'tree hugger, organic, pot-smoking place', I'd start with all-natural beef whenever possible. I went to an organic, natural beef ranch I knew in the British Columbia interior and bought two whole cows. An ambitious endeavour to say the least, but the arrangement was they'd handle working with the processor and storage centre in the lower mainland, who would, in turn, send me small shipments as requested.

My kitchen was prepped and waiting for the delivery of my first natural beef shipment. And then the phone rang. I found out the hard way the beef business was fraught with lessons. The meat processors announced my beef was ready and would arrive today—all of it! *What?* When I asked about the arrangement of small increment deliveries on demand, they informed me they were overrun with business and had no storage space left for my meat. With one freezer for supplies and a small one in the store for the finished product for sale, we had nowhere to store hundreds of pounds of packaged frozen beef. The intention was to add more freezers as the business grew. And that certainly wasn't at the beginning of a start-up—and certainly not today. *Damn!* All the arguing in the world was useless since the truck was already loaded and on its way to the ferry.

So now I learned the value of living in a community where you know a lot of folks. Living rurally, there weren't too many places on the peninsula to buy new freezers on demand, so I talked to friends and neighbours, and searched the local buy and sell. Within hours, I had purchased five second-hand freezers that were delivered or hauled home in my station wagon. Now—stay with me here—remember the description of this property? The old barn sat twenty or so meters from the commercial kitchen and from its days of being used as a sawmill, it was completely wired with a certified heavy-duty electrical box and many plug-in outlets. The health department had no problem with me storing anything frozen in the barn because they were pre-packaged. As long as daily logs were kept on the freezer temperatures, and available for inspection, we were good to go. *A little bit of magic happened that day!*

But the day wasn't over. Later that afternoon, a large truck backed down the driveway and the fun began. Ahh—the lessons I was learning. When you purchase a whole cow, they mean the *whole* cow. You paid for it, you own it—bones and all. Along with hundreds of cuts of beef, we had a large number of packaged bones as well, taking up their own freezer space. Of course, I wanted some for making broths and gravies. *But*, I saw another sideline to rid ourselves of the bulk of meat cuts and bones and make a few dollars. We placed a new sign on North Road, advertising the sale of natural beef cuts and bones for dog owners. In a matter of days, we were down to manageable supplies and took down the sign.

The meat pies would be available in an individual 5-inch pie, a hungry-man deep-dish 6-inch pie, a 10-inch family pie, and a 12-inch party pie. Back in the day, when I catered out of the Roberts Creek Legion, I'd experimented with a 4-inch for seniors. Because they were made in a small tin, there was no bottom pastry, so they became a pot pie offering. But the seniors complained there wasn't enough pastry on a 4-inch tin, and they'd rather buy a 5-inch or a deep-dish pie and share it. Learning my lesson, I scrapped the idea of reviving them.

I found a great wholesaler on the mainland where I could buy bulk pie tins, commercial-sized plastic wrap, boxes of pure lard (about sixty pounds), ten-kilogram bags of unbleached flour, and more. A day trip to Vancouver on the ferry was always a pleasurable outing I enjoyed when necessary.

We were ready to get serious.

Chapter 8

Build a Field and They Will Come...

My doors were open for business, and 'open soon' became 'open'. I placed an ad in the local paper, mailed out flyers, and pinned posters on bulletin boards. And the local tongue wags placed bets on whether anyone would travel down the dirt driveway to no-man's-land. The first few who ventured in laughed when they finally reached their destination, making jokes about wondering what they'd find at the end of the 'yellow brick road' or the 'road to nowhere', and of course, there were Sweeney Todd references. So, I made a few signs to hang on the trees along the way, such as, 'you're on the right track', 'keep going', and 'you're almost there'.

. . .

Pieman

Word began to spread about the little country pie shop, and business increased. It may have been a long drive into the pie shop, but we sat on the main thoroughfare from the ferry terminal, for locals, people who were heading up coast, or north to the next ferry to Powell River. Vacationers on their way to summer cabins and campers loved to pick up fresh pies made that day for dinner, or frozen foods to stock up. Commuters travelling home on a Friday night ferry stopped to pick up dinner, appreciating a no-cook evening. A couple of high school teachers in Gibsons, married with teenagers, always treated themselves on Friday evenings with a Papa D Family Pie.

It was happening and I couldn't be more excited. The cars were coming in, and I'll never forget my first full freezer of frozen product was sold out in a few days. With a lot of debt and a head full of doubts, I was happy to see it was going to be successful. And it was only the beginning.

Ever heard that expression, *Be careful what you wish for*? Here I was, with my little home-based kitchen, supposedly working my way toward a retirement business, finding myself so busy but loving the long hours required. The drawback was my wife began pitching in with wrapping and labelling after working her days at the clinic. Her job was going well, but bus transportation was limited. I decided to drive her to work in the mornings. The thirty-minute drive in gave us a chance to breathe, talk with each other (something we needed with our busy work schedules), and enjoy the beautiful drive through the rain forest of Roberts Creek, the Oceanside drive along the Davis Bay seaside, and then up the hill into picturesque Sechelt to the clinic. At the end of her day, she'd take the bus home. It dropped her at the end of the driveway, and she'd walk the rest of the way in.

After dropping her off at the clinic, the drive home

gave me a chance to think about the business and what my plan for the day would be. Long term, I knew I couldn't take advantage of June's supportive nature and gave thought to a part-time employee. We weren't quite there yet, but close.

The primary benefit to running your own business was and is independence, not having to answer to a direct boss. But you aren't free of worry, constantly reminded you're tied to rules and regulations—especially with a food business. There is no guarantee of sales, so you must, like sharks, constantly move or you won't survive, and your competition will play hardball. It's a trade-off; you must be strong and disciplined, work long hours for small pay, and that's the reality, period.

But I loved it—the illusion of freedom. In this case, it was turning out to be worth it.

About this time, two magical things happened. The health department was cracking down on entrepreneurs who were making food products at home in their kitchens and selling them to the public. A firecracker of a lady approached me to rent space in my kitchen. She supplied homemade jams and jellies to local stores and was required to prove to the health inspector she was using a certified commercial kitchen to make her products. She didn't need space to store her supplies. She brought them with her and took them away when she was done. All she wanted was a corner to work in and the use of a stove top. We made a sweetheart of a deal, where she could use the kitchen a few days a week in exchange for working for me when needed. My second future tenant came knocking on the door a short time later, also looking to use my kitchen. She too had been singled out by the health inspector for running her business out of her kitchen. She was an amazing lady, a licensed practitioner of Chinese medicine. She was looking for some shelves to store her herbal ingredients and a counter to prep her medicine with a press machine. I offered her a corner in the back storeroom, giving her shelf space and a worktable for her press machine. We agreed on a rental price, and she signed a monthly lease agreement. In the end, the two ladies, the health inspector, and I became a happy foursome.

Winter was coming and planning began for Christmas sales and advertising.

Chapter 9

Critters

As we progressed into fall, we soon learned running a business in a pristine, rural part of nature, especially a food business came with some hiccups. It was inevitable we would intertwine with the wildlife, and it wasn't long before Mother Nature let us know we were on her turf.

Let me start with the smaller critters. We put a couple of our own on the payroll and they proved their weight in gold. Marbles was a calico cat who definitely ruled the roost. She was a diva who accepted Picasso, our grey tabby as long as he knew his place and understood she was the boss.

Marbles

There were feral cats in our part of the neighbourhood, but in no uncertain terms would Marbles allow them on our land. She seemed to know the boundaries and chased them off. She was an avid hunter to the point, I'd say, she lived to hunt. Every morning, I'd open both doors to the commercial kitchen and she would do a walk-through from the store to the back storeroom, sniffing in every corner. In one door and out the other, we never had a mouse problem in the kitchen, and believe me, the surrounding fields were full of field mice. Marbles would spend hours perched on the barn roof with her front paws and head hanging over the edge. She'd stare at the back acreage of our neighbour for any movement in the grass and bushes. Once she homed in on a mouse, she was down from the roof, across the dirt driveway, and chasing mice in our neighbour's field.

Picasso

Picasso wasn't a hunter. A gentle, loving soul, he'd make friends with any type of critter. His role was distinctively different from Marbles. He never entered the kitchen, choosing instead to spend the day on the deck beside the door, keeping me company. His self-designated job was to greet the customers, who enjoyed stroking his soft fur; his loving purrs brought some solace to their busy day.

We had raccoons living nearby and Marbles allowed them to walk through the property, but nothing came into our residence without her approval. We had a pet door that was left open in the daytime, but our cats preferred to be inside at night, sharing our bed. So, we'd lock the pet door overnight to keep out unwanted visitors. One evening, as June and I were watching television, with the two cats curled up beside us on the couch, a noise by the door caught our attention. We hadn't yet locked the pet door for the night. The cats' heads popped up, and we all stared at the pet door. A mother racoon and three babies poked their heads through and stared at the cat bowls on the kitchen floor. Marbles gave them a hiss and off they went, running into the dense brush and down to the creek.

Coyote packs were a common sight in our neck of the woods. They followed Gibsons Creek and at night we could hear them yipping, and when one caught dinner, they called out to the others. Cats were a prime choice for dinner, which was another reason we locked our cats in at night. Not that they're easy to catch. Believe it or not, most cats can outrun a coyote, and usually, they fall prey to one only when caught off guard. If Marbles and Picasso sensed danger they ran like hell to the barn, where there was a slight indentation in the ground under the doors. Under they'd go, finding safety where larger animals couldn't follow.

Now, there was one occasion where we almost lost Marbles. We had scheduled her to be spayed at the local vet clinic, and the day before her appointment, she disappeared for a couple of days. She came home pregnant. The vet told us to let her have her kittens and bring her in once she stopped lactating. That became the plan. Well, she was only a few weeks away from giving birth when June and I headed up north to attend our son's wedding. The jam lady was looking after our place, and she drove in one morning to find Marbles frozen to the spot in fear. She knew something was up, and as she rounded the commercial kitchen, there was a coyote in attack mode. It was obvious a chase was about to begin and considering the cumbersome weight of Marble's pregnancy, she'd never have outrun the coyote, nor could she have squeezed her engorged body under the barn door to safety.

The jam lady chased the coyote away and Marbles headed back to the safety of the house.

Pieman

We made a secure, quiet place for Marbles to have her kittens near the woodstove in the house, and she slept there once in a while like she knew it was hers. Picasso kept his distance from her in those last weeks and seemed to sense the quiet space was not meant for him. One night we went to bed and Marbles joined us on the bed. Both cats knew they could sleep at the bottom of the bed but weren't allowed further up, but on this occasion, Marbles wanted to sleep between us. Suspecting her time was close, we let her settle halfway up the bed. About six in the morning, she kicked my wife awake with her back legs. We knew it was her time and she allowed June to carry her to her new bed. Marbles settled right in and let her sit close and stroke her body. June spoke to her quietly, and we watched her give birth to four beautiful kittens—two orange tabbies, one calico, and one male tabby. The next day, to our surprise, another kitten popped out—pure black. We made sure there were no more kittens to be born and a healthy male joined the other four. Marbles was a great mother, doting on her babies. When the time was right, we were able to find good homes for all five kittens. And we had Marbles spayed this time. No more surprises.

We'd found a sense of peace, living with the smaller critters we shared the land with. Even Marbles became accepting of the racoons and squirrels living in our area. Both cats developed a strong sense of awareness when the coyotes were around and stayed away from their hunting grounds down by the creek.

The deer were very prolific. Marbles tolerated does and fawns, but she seemed to have an aversion to the bucks. Maybe, it had something to do with their antler racks. One day, two young bucks munched their way around our field in front of the commercial kitchen. Marbles took exception to them and decided they needed to be run off. She was a great hunter of mice, but for bigger animals that stood taller than her, her orange and white fur did not blend well in the green grasses. They knew she was stalking them and ignored her. As she got closer and started to hiss, they kept an eye on her, moving away from her annoying antics. Marbles decided it was time to pounce, and they decided to teach her a lesson.

They chased her across the field and under an Adirondack chair. They stood on either side butting the chair while Marbles cowered underneath. Their mission to discourage her from bothering them finished, they went back to the field and continued their meal. From that day forward Marbles 'allowed' them to visit whenever they wanted—and wisely ignored them.

Chapter 10

'Big' Critters

OUR PRISTINE RURAL SETTING, WITH ITS FALL COLOURS, came with the largest glitch of all—namely bears. Adapting to living with bears was a one-way street. They came when they wanted, did what they wanted, whenever they wanted. They were definitely unpredictable, and their personalities varied. Some were skittish and ran on sight, others were curious and checked out everything, while a few were bold and no amount of shouting, banging, or honking car horns would make them leave. And of course, mama bears who wandered onto the property with their cubs were the most unpredictable. The two most predominant seasons for sharing our property with bears were spring and fall. In the spring, they had babies with them and came hungry, and the fall season brought them in search of leftover berries and fruit tree offerings, to fatten up for hibernation. Papa D's Meat Pies opened in September, just in time for foraging visitors. What better food to attract bears than the succulent smell of baking meat pies? We'd ordered a large steel commercial dumpster for our kitchen garbage, believing it would be strong enough to withstand the bears. *Wrong!*

It wasn't long before a large bear we nicknamed, 'Arnold Schwarzenegger' paid us a night visit—a bear so strong, he lifted the lid with ease so high that we were left with an annoying yard clean-up to start our next morning. A trip to the hardware store for a hefty padlock came next and I felt confident. I retired that night saying, "There, Arnold, try this." And try he did. With no effort at all, he bent the corner of the steel lid like it was a piece of cardboard, grabbing a couple of garbage bags and frog-marching them over the bank and down to the creek.

I contacted the disposal company and they suggested exchanging the metal dumpster for a couple of portable ones on wheels and locking them in the barn with the freezers. We did and you guessed it, Arnold came back, creating a horrendous racket banging on the barn doors, obviously frustrated by the dirty trick we'd played on him. He came to visit regularly over the next few months, sniffing around the barn, and always left a few claw marks on the door, adding to the previous ones. His efforts to break in were feeble now; a couple of scratches down the door and off he'd go to forage elsewhere.

As the business grew, I found ways to cool my many batches of pies, to either keep fresh for daily customers or freeze for those who bought in bulk. I purchased another fridge and placed it on the deck by the store door. I filled it with fresh pies to keep cool during the day only until June or I were ready to wrap and label them. I'd strapped the fridge to secure it. One particularly busy day, I forgot there were still some pies in the deck fridge and called it a day. *Yup, stupid me!*

Most of the bears were timid, and when I saw them, I'd bang on a pot and off they'd run back down to the creek. All the animals followed the water, and if it wasn't for the smell of baking pies, most would rarely find their way up the bank to our place. So—along came 'Arnold', and he tore the fridge door right off its hinges. He ate the pies, leaving empty tins all over the deck and yard. *One (or many pies) for Arnold! Zero for me!* A lesson well learned on my part. We appeared to be tolerating each other until winter set in and Arnold moved up into the mountains to hibernate.

Our neighbour reported to us that one evening he watched a large bear forage under an apple tree behind his house for the fallen fruit. He'd been away and hadn't yet picked up the blowdowns, which always attract the bears in the fall: easy pickings for them. Now, the problem with rotting apples is that they ferment and if a bear eats enough of them, he becomes a drunken bear. Our neighbour watched the bear pig out on the fallen fruit and begin to stagger. The large animal attempted to climb into the tree, eventually making his way up to a large branch where he passed out. The next morning, the bear was still there, straddled along the branch with all four legs hanging loosely over the sides.

One day, the following spring, I drove June to work and when I returned, there was a mama bear with cubs in the yard. I needed to go into the house before opening the pie shop, but no amount of honking or yelling would move her away. And so, I sat, putting my seat back and turning up the tunes while waiting her out. Eventually, she moved around the side of the house into the forest, and I cautiously left my car and bounded up the stairs into the house.

Pieman

The picture window in the living room looked directly into the forest. I stood for a time watching the cubs play, and their mama forage in the foliage. She chased her cubs up a tree while she grubbed in the grass and the cubs eventually fell asleep in the tree. My first bear family for the season stayed there all day with Mama eventually finding a spot to curl up and sleep. I went to work in my kitchen, cautiously aware of their presence. Since June was due home on the bus that day, I drove down the driveway and met her on the road, not wanting her to walk down that long distance alone. We came into the house and went straight to the picture window. Mama was foraging for food again while the cubs played peek-a-boo from the tree. One popped its head around the side of the tree trunk and finding us watching from our living room, ducked back behind the tree. The other one peeked from the other side, copying its sibling's antics, much to our amusement and entertainment. The bear family was still there when we went to bed, leaving us sometime during the night.

June, who'd always been a city girl, adjusted to rural

life and loved it—but not the bears. She had a love/hate relationship with them. One evening, she was in the commercial kitchen wrapping pies while I was away on the mainland, taking a late ferry home. Arnold came sniffing around the deck and wouldn't leave. There was nothing available for him to eat, and June figured eventually he'd wander off as he usually did. She waited and waited to no avail. It was dusk and she wanted to get across the compound and into the house before dark. She knew Arnold wouldn't leave until he was good and ready, having never responded to pot banging or yelling to move him along. He appeared to know his size and strength allowed him to do as he pleased. So, she waited. Then he began peering in the windows at her. No problem, since the windows were barred. No access there. The two doors to the commercial kitchen were steel doors that opened outwards. No way could he push his way through the doors, she thought, and momentarily felt safe inside. But he soon let her know he wanted in. He began sniffing around the door and when he stood to his full height and pushed and snorted against it, she panicked. Alone, with visions of what he'd done in the past to the fridge door on the deck, and the steel lid on the dumpster, she ran to the storage room, locked herself in the bathroom and called 911.

Now you have to understand, that in those days, Gibsons had one RCMP officer on duty for the evening/night shift. Dispatch at the local office closed at suppertime and calls were transferred to Vancouver on the mainland. There wasn't a lot of crime in those days and the Staff Sergeant was hard-pressed to write up incident reports for his column in the weekly newspaper. I remember one weekly report in the paper that read like this:

Pieman

Police were sent out on a disturbance call at 3 a.m. Friday to Lower
Road in Roberts Creek, only to discover a burning running shoe in the
middle of the road. Fire fighters soon distinguished the flames. Police have no
witnesses to the crime and to date, no one has laid claim to the shoe.

So, here's June, trying to explain to a big city dispatcher that she's trapped in a rural commercial kitchen, with a bear trying to break in, and she needs the officer on duty to come to her rescue so she could lock up and cross the compound to the house. She was told the officer was busy at the moment and would get there when he could.

Finally, Arnold left the deck and June couldn't see him anywhere. She ventured onto the deck and peered around the corner in time to see his back end lumbering down the driveway. She locked up the kitchen, ran like hell to the safety of the house, and called Vancouver dispatch to cancel her call for help.

About halfway up our long driveway, there's a huge thicket of blackberry bushes running about twenty feet on both sides. In August, we'd pick them and make blackberry jam. Neighbours would come and pick the berries as well. If the birds didn't get the remainder, there were still plenty of succulent berries left for the bears to enjoy at the end of August and into September. One evening, June got off the bus, started up the driveway and spotted a bear having his evening meal. Not knowing if it was a skittish animal or an aggressive one, she decided not to try to scare it away since there was nowhere for her to run for safety should he run at her. She backed away and ran over to the neighbour who called me and asked me to drive up to his house and pick her up. I drove the dirt laneway at high speed, honking the horn, and he was gone by the time I reached the berry bushes.

As I said at the beginning of this chapter, living rurally with bears is an adjustment on our part, not theirs. But June was a real trouper and did what she needed to live in peace with them.

Chapter 11

'Tis the Season...

The drive in...

The destination...

SOON THE FIRST HOLIDAY SEASON WAS UPON US, AND THE tourtière orders started to come in. My grandmother, being from England did not have an old family tourtière recipe. Since it was a French-Canadian speciality, popular over the holidays, many folks had family recipes for tourtière and were more than happy to share them with me. I faithfully listened, wrote them down, experimented with some, and eventually settled on one. Tourtière became our favourite Christmas season pie, and we soon discovered the 12" pies were flying out the door as people planned holiday parties and family dinners.

We had acquired a nifty Coldstream three-shelf display cooler, which was always full of fresh-baked pies. We set it up in what was dubbed the smallest store anywhere, by the entrance door. There was a door into the kitchen and an open pass-through in the wall next to the kitchen door. A fridge with additional fresh products sat in the opposite corner to the cooler. Any unsold stock was moved into the freezer under the window in the store for bulk buyers. Between the cooler and the fridge, a table was set up with an antique breadbox we used as a cash register, with a pen and guest book (which people loved to write in).

I was really happy with the response the locals were expressing. I'd set up some local pub trade on a wholesale basis, but customers were visiting the store as well and buying from me directly because there was more variety. The pubs and stores took only basic meat and chicken stock, while my little store at one time offered up to fourteen different types of pies. I still had remnants of my catering business from my old Roberts Creek days, and it was a lucrative addition to my pie business. One annual event was the riding club (horsey set) that ran an annual foxhunt. One year, in particular, stands out because it was held during the worst rainstorm I'd ever seen. We set up outside under the tents amidst much laughter. The riders returned soaked and muddy, but they sat down for the banquet in high spirits anyway.

There was an indigenous band from Powell River who bought bulk for families and friends, (they couldn't get enough 5-inch ground beef and onion pies). We supplied some B&Bs, and a music festival purchased three hundred pies and sold them all.

The Christmas season was a resounding success, and the meat pie business was a growing enterprise. It was hard work, but having a high-energy, type-A personality, I thrived on it, enjoyed the work, and decided to add to my product line. More about that later.

Store before the display cooler was purchased.

Since I worked alone most of the time and needed to make trips to town for supplies, there were times when the store had to be closed until I returned. Part-timers weren't always available when I needed to be away. The store wasn't at the level of affording full-time staff and closing the store was costing me business. Sooo…I decided to operate the same way as local free-range egg and flower stands. I placed a sign on the antique bread box, *'Help yourself and leave your money in the breadbox! Write your order down in the guest book and your payment amount!'*

That's right—the honour system! A lot of people

thought I was crazy for invoking the honour system on occasions when no one was around. But at that time, I chose to put my faith in humanity and trust my fellow man. And you know what? It worked. People loved it. Not once, did any strangers who departed the ferry from the big city and stopped in for pies or any down-on-their-luck locals ever stiff me. I'm a strong believer in what goes around, comes around. I trusted them, and they thanked me for it with their business and honesty.

Some comments from our guest book: (Using their initials, no full names)

Sep 2003
Vancouver should have pies this good!
Nicely seasoned and the best pastry!
PW, North Lake

Sep 2005
Papa D you've done it!! Thrilled with your pies. We have a B&B on
Vancouver Island and will email you for an order.
LG & DG, Mill Bay

Nov 2005 - Hi you two,
Thanks again for the 'help yourself' honour system. The television I took last time isn't working, so I took your new one, plus your couch, and a Camino painting. If you get anything else new, please call me. I hate having to take chances on old stuff. Oh, and took some pies too!
Adios, D & L, Madeira Park

Chapter 12

All About Me...

AT THIS POINT, HOPEFULLY, WITHOUT SOUNDING LIKE A self-absorbed narcissist, I want to explain a little about why I felt this book was important for me to write and share. I was born with a strong need to escape from what I believed was the banality of everyday life, which of course led me on a search for how best to achieve that. Being an artist and a dreamer, and coming from the '50s era, without a strong male influence in my life to guide me into adulthood, some of my many business endeavours and personal relationships did not always lead me to success by societal standards.

I know who my real father is, but he never factored into my life. My first stepfather married my mother when she was pregnant with me. He was around long enough to get my mother pregnant two more times before he fell on the wrong side of the law and disappeared from our lives. There were four of us, myself (the eldest), my brother, and two younger sisters when stepfather number two came along. We all moved to a big old house on Mission Hill in Vernon, and my first memory of my new stepfather was him calling my brother and me outside in a snowstorm. We were told to climb a ladder onto the roof, and we couldn't come down until all the snow was shovelled off. He'd removed the ladder and we had to find another way down. He believed we needed toughening up, and this was our first lesson. My fearless brother jumped off the roof into a snow bank that had accumulated at one end of the house. To him, it was great fun—but not me. I think that's when I became afraid of heights. He finally coaxed me into jumping, which eventually I did. Yup, our new dad was a mean son-of-a-bitch. I'd learned to stay out of his way, which was what he wanted anyway until he needed us to do the chores. I could gauge his moods when he'd come home, especially if he was drinking, and would find a closet to hide in with a stack of books and a flashlight where I'd lose myself in the worlds of other peoples' lives. I'm sure he knew where I was, but he left me alone because it fed his need for control, and he thought it was funny. My brother, the fearless one, was the opposite of me. He'd get defiant and stand up to the old man. I got my fair share of whippings, but over the years my poor brother suffered way worse.

I remember a high school counsellor telling me I was highly intelligent, and I needed to go out into the world and find myself, but he wasn't sure if my bohemian way of thinking combined with that intelligence would make me a billionaire—or land me in jail. Such has been my life—not landing in jail or becoming a billionaire, but the push/pull of wanting to chase the almighty dollar or live off the land in blue jeans and bare feet. And so, at various times of my life, I can attest to a journey of doing both.

Luckily, I found in June, my wife of thirty-seven years, a supportive partner who sometimes knows me better than I know myself. And together, we've travelled down many life paths. But here I was at the age of sixty, looking for gainful employment, and wanting another shot at success in my life. Of course, success is relative and means different things to different people. My wife's philosophy has always been, if you have a dream, chase it. If you achieve it, it's a success, and its monetary value isn't relative. You dreamt it, chased it, achieved it —therefore, you're a success. Where did this woman come from?

So here I was baking meat pies, which wasn't discovering a new green energy source (a past endeavour of mine), and I was enjoying it too as well as providing a living for myself to keep us in comfort, combined with my wife's salary. The business was growing but manageable, but still I felt a nagging concern about where I was going with my life.

Art was always a part of my life, since starting art school at the age of six. I always thought of myself as an artist, working in many forms: oils, watercolours, acrylics, and some sculpting. With the business running smoothly, I was painting again, having fixed up a studio in our home with perfect light. The realization finally broke through, that my art was more than pretty or competent, more than scenarios, wildlife, or portraits; no—it was expressionism, it was thought in paint, and it must show thought or an idea that could cause some sort of reaction in the viewer, or at the very least, prompt them to buy it (smiling).

After years of pursuing my artistic endeavours on and off at various times of my life, deep concern was growing in me that there had to be more than just doing art for money or praise, or conveying a message, and I knew deep down that wasn't really what I wanted to do.

Let me delve a little into my psyche here, and say the 'pie thing' was very satisfying in that I was creating something that was appreciated and consumed repeatedly thus needing to be replaced. I was buzzed by the fact I'd created my little enterprise on a previously neglected property, and the praise and support reinforced that I had achieved what I'd been chasing—a successful enterprise and simple rural living—a perfect combination. Plus, my suppliers and customers were becoming friends.

And then, along came the universal problem of ego. Yep, there it was.

I knew if I just stayed the course and worked hard, my simple business could be sufficient. But ahh…here's the rub, I was still troubled with ego, the deep-down feeling that this humble enterprise wasn't enough, constantly looking at what the Germans call 'Weltbild', the big picture.

I was constantly nagged by the thoughts I must do more. I must, after a lifetime of soul searching for the answers to the big questions: Why are we here? How did we get here? Where is this? Where are the boundaries of this universe? And what of religion?

My stepfather was Catholic, and all of us kids attended the Catholic church. My mother ended up with nine children all told because of his religious beliefs. The only thing I enjoyed about church was singing in the choir. I went because I was forced to and even at a young age, the hypocrisy was clear to me. My stepdad was big in the Knights of Columbus, went to every meeting, came home drunk, beat on his family, and Sundays went to confession. He said his Hail Marys and believed he was forgiven for his sins of the week and free to act them out again the next.

Our priest tried hard to convert me to the ways of God by taking me down to the wine cellar to counsel me. He'd sit me in a chair at the end of an aisle with my back to the wall, and place his chair in front of mine, so close our knees touched. He'd lean forward and place his hands on my inner thighs, and when he wanted to make a strong point, he'd squeeze his fingers into my thighs. I remember how sweaty his hands and face would get, and his breath smelled of wine. I'd been physically abused by my stepfather, who I feared, but I wasn't afraid of my priest and would glare back at him defiantly. Maybe that's why it never went any further than that—at least with me. There was gossip in the community, and an incident of a young man firing bullets in the church vestibule during mass one day, but everything was hush-hush in those days. When I was twelve, I took a list of questions to him about God and asked him to answer them. Down we went to the wine cellar and while squeezing my thighs yet again, he gave me the same rhetoric I'd heard before. He then asked me if I was satisfied, and I told him: "No". At that point, he told me I was a fallen Catholic and it was time for me to leave the church and not come back until I'd found God. He was sure I'd be back one day—he and God would accept me back into the fold. I left elated with the news but scared to death of what my stepfather would say. When I told him I was banished from the church, he stared at me long and hard—then he laughed. He was unpredictable that way; if I thought he'd be furious with me and expected a beating, he'd laugh, or if I expected he'd find something I did was funny, he'd blow up and I'd brace myself for what was coming next.

In 2015 when the movie, Spotlight premiered, June and I went to see it. At the end of the movie, the audience was in total silence. No one got up to leave during the credits, which wasn't the norm. The audience sat through the long credits in total silence, all of us lost to our thoughts—and of course, my mind was in the wine cellar with our priest. I squeezed my wife's hand so tight that it hurt. But she never said a word until later. When the theatre finally emptied and we went to our car, I locked eyes with the man parked next to us. We stood by our cars and stared at each other in silence, sensing each other's emotions. Finally, he said, "We had one of them at my church."

"We did too," I replied. We nodded to each other in understanding and got into our cars. It was one of those poignant moments in life when two strangers knew they were sharing something in common that didn't require words.

I never told anyone about my visits to the wine cellar and certainly, my stepfather would never have believed his spiritual leader might be bent. I felt sure it would only bring on a beating. My problem with the Catholic church is this: Are all priests sexual abusers? Of course not. But part of the atrocity is the fact that the church covered it up, moving the accused to other parishes where they had access to new victims. There's no reconciliation for that kind of behaviour in my books.

And here we are in the present day, facing the past atrocities of the churches, not just the Catholic diocese, as well as the role played by the government regarding residential schools and the treatment of innocent, indigenous children torn away from their families in our country. At the time of writing this chapter, the Vatican still hadn't offered an apology. A year later, the Pope finally apologized and denounced the events that happened at residential schools as genocide. I suppose it's a step towards healing, but words can't undo what has already been done.

Decades later, I forgave my stepfather for all of it (for my benefit, not for his), and had worked my way at least to an understanding of how to deal with organized religions, arriving at a place influenced by Simone Weil's statement that we should 'live by the light of our own mind'.

I tell you all of this as an explanation as to why I preferred to be my own boss in life and why the thought of being an entrepreneur had such strong appeal. I came to recognize my subconscious need to be a manic overachiever throughout my life and finally understood how my childhood influenced my life decisions.

If you think, dear reader, I'm about to espouse some

mind-blowing new philosophy or religion, nope. I'm only explaining my state of mind at the time, which will come into play further into the book. But let me say, in no small way was I losing enthusiasm for my baking and selling my creations. On the contrary—I was just dealing with my own insecurities: aka ego.

Chapter 13

Art=Creation, Creation=Comfort Foods, Comfort Foods=Art...

WITH THE SUCCESS OF THE PIES, TWO THINGS EVOLVED IN the business. One was the addition of more savoury pies, the likes of which had never been seen before—or so I've been told. The second is the addition of other comfort food products.

I mentioned earlier that at one time we offered 14 types of savoury pies. Adding to the basic chicken deluxe, beefsteak, steak and kidney, ground beef and onion, and ground beef and veggies, I began to experiment. The Christmas favourite, tourtière, was developed from the original ground beef and onion base. Next was turkey with vegetables, pork pies, and a vegetarian pie consisting of cheese and onion which was very popular, followed by a chilli pie, a chicken fajita pie, and a Tex-Mex pie made from the beef and onion base. Our biggest sellers were curried chicken with mandarin orange and my famous cowboy pie.

June pushed me into the curried chicken with mandarin orange. I had my doubts, but it became a big seller. So, credit goes to her for that one. The cowboy pie was a novel idea, created one day when customers said there couldn't possibly be any more varieties. I mused about one more pie addition. I wanted to create my own version of a Canadian pie like the French Canadian tourtière; something hearty that would satisfy a cowboy sitting around the campfire. (I told you I was a dreamer.) Using the basic ground beef and onion recipe, I added baked beans, bacon, and a dollop of real maple syrup for that Canadian touch—adding a horseshoe-shaped piece of pastry on top. Customers loved it, especially the men, and it became one of my most prolific sellers.

As popular as the pies had become, there were actually people who didn't like pastry (hard to imagine, right?), and there were those who couldn't eat pastry for health reasons. My customers brought me stories of friends and family members who loved my fillings but threw away the pastry. This got me thinking I needed to be more creative and add new products to my menu. So, along came the 'Potato Toppers', a loaf pan filled with my best-selling pie fillings, topped with a hefty serving of mashed potatoes. My chilli pies were sold simply as 'chilli', no pastry.

Some of my steady customers were labourers who loved to eat one of my meat pies on lunch break. They had no problem eating them cold, as they had no access to microwaves or ovens, but they complained about the awkwardness of eating out of a pie tin, as opposed to eating hand-held foods like sandwiches. Sooo—I made sausage rolls.

Then, I remembered my Nana telling me that when they cooked on the ranch for the workers who couldn't come in to eat, how she'd made them pocket pies. They carried them out on the range in their pockets and pulled them out when they were hungry. The pocket pie my Nana made copied the Cornish pie previously created for use by miners who carried them in their pockets deep below ground to eat during breaks. My brain worked overtime on the memory and soon I'd added 'Fort McLeod Hand Pies' to my menu.

One group of customers who came in steadily, by word of mouth were 'Aussie' travellers. I loved the Aussies and the Kiwis, who all seem to have a great sense of humour. Meat pies are a popular staple in Australia and New Zealand, and did they love their meat pies! They'd travel from the lower mainland to our peninsula by ferry, stop in for a pie, head up to Powell River on a second boat, and cross over to Vancouver Island on a third ferry. No hand pies for them. They'd fold my pies in half and eat them cold right out of the tin. It was always a joy to spend some time jawing with them and hearing their humorous travel stories.

So here it was—the realization of a dream, no matter how small, partially due to a saying I'd read on the back of a matchbox: *If a person would be content with smaller ambitions, the chances of success were greater*. I'd been troubled with lofty ideas and endeavours for years, wanting to be Steve Jobs, or you know, one of the great ones—and in my artistic efforts, perhaps Jackson Pollock or Bateman.

So you can see, in a way, I was fulfilling my artistic urges with my culinary creations. All those years of practising art prepared me to think outside the box, free my creative juices, and apply my artistic talents to my food products. Who'd have thunk?

Chapter 14

Remembering Lessons Learned...

I SETTLED IN AND WAS VERY MUCH ENJOYING RUNNING THIS little enterprise. Financially and personally, we were set. Now, every business has some concerns and mine were that I'd poison my customers with tainted food or leave a small bone in the fillings that would catch in a customer's throat. Because of those two fears, I made sure to conform to all the health rules. If I found myself in doubt with any product, I threw it out, no question. And I can say that to my knowledge none of my fears came to be.

After our first year in business, my investor came to visit and respecting his privacy, I'll just say that he was having personal and business problems. He asked me if I would give his spouse a job in my kitchen, believing if she had a job to go to, she would settle into life in Canada. I obliged, but it didn't work out because the root of the problem was that she was missing her family in the Netherlands and what she really wanted was to move back to Europe. One Saturday, he visited me to discuss it, and I told him it wasn't workable. I could see he was upset and as he paced back and forth, I let him talk.

Now, that same day, we were hosting an annual party, put on by June's employer. He was also there, setting up for that night's festivities on the lawn. Overhearing some of the conversation, he became concerned I was being pressured into doing something I didn't want to do. Unknown to us, he mulled it over for a few days.

Meanwhile, I informed my investor that I was intractable, and I couldn't allow personal issues to interfere with our arrangement; he accepted that, and the conversation was over. A few days later, June's employer came to us and expressed his concerns for our business. He was willing to buy out our investor in the form of a loan to the business. We discussed it, set the terms, and I worked out a fair buyout with the first investor who thanked me because he gave the money to his wife who took the children and moved back to Europe. He has since moved to Great Britain where he remarried and is raising another family. We've remained in touch to this day and have stayed friends. The business was doing so well at this point, it had no outstanding bills except that one monthly loan payment.

Back to my art. Through the sale of a series of watercolours, an opportunity came to me from an author of a poetry book. He admired my watercolours and had sent one to a friend of his who had a gallery in Los Angeles. The gallery owner told him I was talented and recommended he should contract me to do illustrations for his poems in the book. The author was an Englishman, who lived in Vancouver. Now being the constant dreamer, I was flattered, of course, and we met one day in the city to discuss the book. I told him I'd think about it and get back to him.

Through the years, one thing I learned was not to spread myself too thin. My business was doing well but required my energy and input to stay that way. Oh, I should add at first, he offered me a contract to work on the project, but then, he offered me 50 % of the profits instead. Few poetry books become big sellers in the publishing industry, so doing this book with the author might stroke my ego, but never fill my pockets. Half of nothing is nothing. And my business could suffer. So, I told him I wasn't interested due to time constraints.

A very disgruntled poet called me up and acting very 'Downton Abbey', said: "You're turning down my offer because you want to make 'pies'? This is an opportunity to get into the publishing business. Are you mad?"

I said, "Yes, I guess I am. And guess what? After I've created my product, people consume them and come back for more. Quite unlike the 'Arts', unless you're very lucky."

And then there were more…

Chapter 15

Ob-La-Di, Ob-La-Da...

AND LIFE WENT ON, *BRAH!* I WAS WORKING LONG HOURS and loving what I was doing. My customer base was growing through word of mouth and curiosity. Being consistent was the key. People would drive by my signage for months, hear something from someone, and in they'd come to check it out. Word spread to the city, among ferry travellers passing through or coming to country cottages. And—let's not forget the magic...

Feb, 2003
*Your **Tortiere** pies were a*
huge hit at our wedding. My family all
agree they're the best pies we've ever had!
P.B., Kitimat, BC

Apr, 2003
Best pies I've ever eaten!
J.C., Pitt Meadows, BC

Oct, 2003
You save the day with your pies available in our freezers!
J & S, Davis Bay, BC

July, 2005
Back Again!
M & C, Abbotsford, BC

Aug, 2005
**Hi, Papa D,
1 – 10" Chicken Deluxe**
*Dr. L & D.W.,
Madeira Park, BC*

Apr, 2004
***Thanks so much for the Turkey Pies.
Took 5/$20***
J.H., Gibsons, BC

Aug, 2005
*Dennis, Wonderful Pies, I'm going to order six of the 10"
for a party, took a card,
Will phone you.*
Thx, J.M., Gibsons, BC

July, 2004
*Dennis, took 4 cowboys, 1 chicken deluxe.
Left $20-if I owe more, catch u next time!*
Thx, L., Sechelt, BC

Sep, 2005
*The chicken deluxe 6" deep pie is the best we've ever
eaten, better than White Spot!*
D.W. & J.W., West Vancouver

Oct, 2005
Wow! Love the old country flair!
K.W. & R.W., Kelowna, BC

June V. Bourgo & Dennis Bourgo

Nov, 2005
Thanks for the honour system. Took 5 pies.
(Hid money in jam cabinet)
M.W., Victoria, BC

Jan, 2006
Dennis, They are Great!
We served 8 people with 2 – 10" pies
And they wanted more!!
D & J, Gibsons, BC

Nov, 2005
Yummy in the tummy!
1 Chicken Deluxe Family Pie $16.75
T., Gibsons, BC

Dec, 2005
Hi! First time, recommended by Dr. L & D.
(But I'm not like them. Left your TV.)
Bought 1 family chicken, 5/5"
B.N., Madeira Park, BC

March, 2006
Pre-ordering 2-12" Beefsteak
for next Monday.
Pre-paid, money in bread box!
M.T., Gibsons, BC

May, 2006
Commuting from Horseshoe Bay for
the best chicken pie ever! Keep them
coming, Dennis!
P.W., Halfmoon Bay, BC

June, 2006
Love your Attitude!
C & V, Vancouver, BC

Pieman

July, 2006
Love your pies!
I'm opening a hot & cold lunch truck,
Could you supply me wholesale?
Left my card in the bread box.
The Lunch Lady.
R.D., Gibsons, BC

July, 2006
Travelling through.
Looking forward to eating the
pies tonight.
Love your set up!
M.W. & B.W.
Scottsdale, Arizona

Sep, 2006
Flying to Toronto tomorrow to a
family reunion, taking a
Cowboy family pie with us.
A definite must!
R & S, Gibsons, BC

Aug, 2006
Pie-topia! Love it!
K., N., & E.,
California Travellers

Sep, 2006
Bye, Papa D!
Filled our cooler with pies.
Off to Mexico for the winter.
See you in the spring!
Thanks, G & R
Halfmoon Bay, BC

June V. Bourgo & Dennis Bourgo

Oct, 2006
Dennis...
We love the pies. Please send more
via e-mail (Ha Ha)!
J & C, Edmonton, Alberta

Jan, 2007
Best pies I've ever eaten!
Thank you, Papa D.
M.S.
Visitor from England

Just a select few of the comments left in the guest books over the time Papa D's was in operation. The words and support of all the customers are what kept me going and made the whole experience a fun and successful one.

So there you have it: a small, locally-run enterprise that turned me into a *Pie Star*!

Chapter 16

Work and Play (ne'er the two shall mix)...

ONE OF THE ABSOLUTE PLEASURES OF LIVING WHERE WE DID was living close to our two oldest grandchildren. They would come over on Friday night after school and stay until Saturday evening, and sometimes until Sunday morning. They were eight and ten at the time and all they wanted was to spend fun times with their grandparents. If we had a particularly busy time with our home business, I'd have to put some time in at the pie shop, which did not sit well with them. All they wanted was my time.

With the success of our honour system, I decided I wouldn't work on Saturdays so we could spend the day with the kids. If we left the property, the honour system came into play.

One Friday morning, I got a call from my grandson scheduled to arrive that evening. They were out of school for the day and wanted to come early. Could I pick up him and his sister? Of course, I did, with the understanding I'd had a full bake day the day before and needed to clean the kitchen. They had to amuse themselves for about an hour while I finished up. June was at work in Sechelt, so they were on their own. They asked if they could use scrap lumber and plywood stored in the old barn to build a fort between a large old doghouse and a tree. They intended to hide behind it and watch for the deer that frequented our place during the day.

As I washed pots in the commercial kitchen, I kept an eye on them through the window. I finished my pots and changed the water to finish up with some baking trays. As the deep sink started to fill, I saw them carrying an old wooden toboggan over to their fort and smiled at their imaginative skills of using it to fill the gaps in the walls. Little did I know how far they had stretched their imagination. They disappeared behind the doghouse and the next thing I knew, shrill screams came from my granddaughter, followed by the fearful, panicked voice of my grandson yelling my name.

"Papa D, Papa D, help!"

Now, anyone who has spent time around children comes to recognize the degrees and levels of screams depicting excitement, play, anger, or fear. Theirs told me they were in big trouble, and I was out the door and running across the yard to their makeshift fort—but they weren't there.

I could hear them both screaming my name on the path leading down the bank to Gibsons Creek. I found my grandson lying in the middle of a prickle bush, unable to climb out. I pulled him out and onto his feet to the haunting shriek of my granddaughter, Haley, further down the trail. Without waiting for an explanation, I slid down the very steep, muddy pathway.

Remember the story at the beginning of this book, about the original Norwegian owners of the acreage who'd built a spa in the bank, sat in there with hot rocks in the middle of winter, and jumped into the cold pond naked? I found my granddaughter hanging onto a tree branch over that pond, the lower part of her body submerged in the icy water. Rest assured, if she'd fallen into the pond, it wasn't deep enough for her to drown in; unless she knocked herself unconscious and slipped under the water. I pushed the what-ifs from my mind and lifted her back onto the ground.

The facts of what happened? They scrapped the idea of using the toboggan as part of their fort walls in a matter of seconds when they decided it would be cool to sit on it and slide down the bank on the slippery mud path to the creek. Being protective of his sister, my grandson sat her in front and climbed on the back behind her to hold her in place. Once it took on a life of its own, with no way of controlling the speed, he'd yelled at her to bail. He did—landing in the prickle bush. She didn't—clinging to the toboggan, frozen in place until it left the pathway and headed for the pond. We never did find the toboggan, believing it had flown over the pond, travelled on to the creek below and floated downstream.

I took them into the house and told them to strip and take a hot shower. It was a cold day, and they were both muddy and my granddaughter, of course, was wet and shivering. As soon as I mentioned the shower, a bell went off. "Oh shit," I yelled and took off running to the commercial kitchen. I re-entered the kitchen to a floor covered with hot, soapy water and ran to the sink to turn off the faucet I'd left running when switching roles from dishwasher to knight in shining armour.

After I'd cleaned up the floor, I left the pans to soak in the sink and returned to the house. If the health inspector made a surprise visit and issued a citation for leaving pans in the sink, so be it. (In reality, I was pretty sure he'd never show up on a Friday, and believe it or not, he always called me a couple of days ahead and warned me he was coming. All good.) Their clothes were put in a wash cycle, and I found them showered and sitting on the couch looking quite contrite. I couldn't believe I'd been watching them from the window and yet, they'd still been able to pull off a dangerous stunt right in front of my eyes. All the what-ifs I'd pushed aside earlier came back as I lectured them on their bad choice. They begged me not to tell their parents what they'd done. I mulled that over and decided it was probably in *my* best interest as well as theirs to keep it our little secret. After all, I was in the kitchen working for an hour, and even if I could keep an eye on them, I'd likely be accused by a frightened parent of not being diligent. So, we made a pact to never tell anyone (except June) if they promised not to do anything that stupid again. The reason, I'm telling you this story in the life of being a grandparent is because I made a pact with myself to never work when they were over, even for a short hour. And this story comes into play in another way, later on in the story.

Chapter 17

Fifteen minutes of fame...

A LITTLE OVER TWO YEARS IN, WE WERE ENJOYING OUR rural lifestyle and things were running smoothly. June had dropped to three days a week with the clinic and worked some hours with me in the kitchen. On the last day of October 2004, an article appeared in the Sunday edition of the *Vancouver Province* about hidden treasures on the Sunshine Coast, which included an esoteric two-sentence mention of Papa D's Meat Pies. The writer wrote about a winding trail to a place where you can buy meat pies and farm-fresh eggs (yes, we'd added eggs to our products) and payment was on the honour system. The idea of adding free-range eggs to our offerings came easy since I knew it would add country charm to Papa D's.

Years ago, when we lived in Roberts Creek, we had a chicken coop with a couple of dozen hens. There's nothing better than farm-fresh eggs for breakfast, and June sold the excess to people she worked with in the city. At the end of the school year, an elementary school teacher asked if we would like to add four chickens to our brood from a school project he'd run for the year with his students. The day he delivered them, we were away, and he dropped them in the yard. We returned home to find two new hens and two roosters—not what we'd expected. Now those roosters were ornery and tried to rule the roost way beyond the hens. My daughter had two horses and one morning she bent over a barrel for some grain and the two roosters came running. One jumped on her back and began biting her neck, while the other attacked her calves. Once we calmed her down, the roosters were donated to our neighbour's stew pot—but not before they'd fertilized the hens' eggs.

We had a problem with a neighbour's dog, an Australian blue heeler who would continuously escape his property and kill some of our chickens, much to our annoyance. A few days after the roosters became dinner, most of the hens disappeared. We thought the dog had killed them. Then, one Saturday morning while sitting around the breakfast table, we heard a strange noise that got louder. Our daughter shrieked: "Oh my God, look!"

We followed her gaze to the side door to the house which opened into the laundry room. It was wide open as it was already a hot summer morning. The wooden deck, which measured about four feet by three feet was covered with a yellow mass of squirming, chirping, baby chicks. The hens had taken to the bush to lay their fertilized eggs and nurture them, all of them returning with their brood at the same time. All our efforts to protect them inside the coop, including wire fencing that went deep in the ground to keep critters from digging underneath, sadly failed. One night, two weasels found a way in and killed them all. We lost most of our chickens over the next year either from ageing out or because of the damn heeler.

The next summer we had one lonely chicken left, whom we dubbed Mrs Chicken. She faithfully gave us one egg a day. The neighbour down the road had moved on along with his dog, so we expected she could live out her life in peace. One weekend, our eight-year-old niece arrived. Remembering all the eggs she'd collected the last time she'd visited, she excitedly asked me if she could collect the eggs. I told her we only had Mrs Chicken and pickings would be scarce. Off she ran to the coop, unaware that the night before I had bought a dozen eggs at the corner store while she was sleeping and placed them in Mrs Chicken's favourite roosting spot. Tamara found the hen happily roosting on the bonanza eggs, which must have shocked the chicken. I must have messed up the hen's psyche. My niece came running back yelling: "Jackpot! Jackpot! Uncle Dennis, I need a bowl."

I tried to explain that a chicken can only lay one egg a day and she didn't need a bowl. Finally, disgusted with me, she ran back to the coop and after a battle with Mrs Chicken, who did not want to give up her eggs, she rolled up the bottom of her shirt and filled it with the eggs. Tamara walked carefully back with the eggs in tow, proving to me she was right, and I was wrong.

I think she was in her teens before I told her what I'd done.

But I digress, so back to my fifteen minutes of fame. Little did I know those two sentences in the Vancouver Sunday paper would start a chain reaction of events that would bring me more business and take me down a new road of thought concerning my little country store.

My initial thought about this small note of appreciation for my meat pies was no one would ever see it, but I soon learned not to underestimate the power of a Sunday morning Vancouver newspaper read over a relaxing cup of coffee. My second thought was the biggest open-kept secret regarding Papa D's (the honour system —take what you want and leave your money) had just been printed in a big-city newspaper. *Ouch!* Visions of unsavoury big-city gangstas ransacking my kitchen and store filtered through my mind. Maybe I'd have to rethink this honour system thing, which had become an established part of Papa D's and a big part of its country charm and appeal.

What did happen, was it got the attention of a local writer. He wrote a column for the *Coast Independent* from 1997 to 2001, and then he worked with the *Coast Reporter*. His bi-monthly column, *Sunshine Sketches* provided a historical and current look into life on the Sunshine Coast and the locals loved his depictions in the form of sketches and stories. His column was a popular read in the community newspaper.

June and I were interviewed and on November 26, 2004, Papa D's was featured in *Sunshine Sketches*. This was the best advertising a small business owner could have. Papa D's was 'discovered' all over again.

I just noticed for the first time looking at his sketch, he included the infamous toboggan leaning up against the building, which disappeared forever through the adventures of my grandkids as told in the previous chapter.

In March 2005, he published what was to be his last book of three, *Last of the Sunshine Sketches, A Final Collection of Drawings and Stories about BC's Beautiful Sunshine Coast*. He'd asked my permission to print the newspaper story of Papa D's in the book. Now, the timing is a bit confusing for some, as he indexed it in the list of stories from the 1980s, which was when I started baking my meat pies under my contract with the Roberts Creek Legion (remember back then?) and my little country store wasn't opened until 2002. But Papa D's was immortalized into the history of the coast and I couldn't be happier.

Chapter 18

To Grow or Not To Grow...

At this point, we're in our third year, and I'd been receiving enquiries about franchising. That's right, franchising Papa D's. There was a butcher shop in Victoria on Vancouver Island that was famous for its meat pies. Two of our customers lived in Victoria but came to their summer home on the Sunshine Coast regularly. Every time they stopped in for pies, they pushed me to consider opening a franchise in Victoria because in their opinion mine were better than the local butcher's pies. I was flattered but declined—still the seed was planted. Then a serious enquiry arrived from some folks in Powell River at the north end of the Sunshine Coast. So, I gave it some serious thought but held off on making a decision. Call it maturity, or simply my age questioning if I had the energy it would take to carry this out, but I found myself leaning towards a much, simpler life.

I'd already spent so much of my life searching for the fame and fortune that so many of us seek and was realizing what a mug's game this was. Our time on this planet is so limited and precious.

During the many hours spent alone in my kitchen doing the rote work of baking, I had lots of time to examine my life and carefully contemplate my remaining time on this planet. I thought often of my grandparents, and what a life they'd had, leaving England in their teens on an arduous boat trip with limited funds to become indentured servants in Canada to pay off their passage, which led them west to homestead on the Old Man River at Fort McLeod.

The indentured servant thing is little known in Canada—I don't recall being taught anything about this in school. They were debt slaves and had to serve as servants and other occupations to repay these debts for as long as ten years. Not unlike a lot of folks who work at servile jobs to pay car payments, mortgages, or high-interest credit card debt today.

My grandfather, who lived to ninety-five, was indentured to the church and was tasked with a censorship editing position, reading books in search of anything considered improper for good Christians to read. He told me once, after a long pull on his ever-present pipe, "Denny, I'm not a fan of religion after the years involved with that church, and I have little time for that nonsense." That started me into a life-long search to discover for myself what to believe in, and not just the spiritual side of life.

If you saw the movie *Missouri Breaks*, there's a bonfire scene where Randy Quaid's character, a country bumpkin type of cowboy, is sitting with Marlon Brando's arrogant character who sarcastically asks Quaid how his life's going. He hesitates and pokes the fire, and says, "Life is not like anything I ever seen before."

This has always been my philosophy. I was never able to accept just working and getting 'stuff' as enough to fulfil me. I recognized that a lot of people were satisfied as long as they were getting the 'stuff' they wanted, and they had no problem with the mystery of life, never seeming to question, or leaving the questions up to the religions they'd been indoctrinated in since childhood. More on this later.

As for the business, for sure it would have been nice

to hire a full-time assistant or two, find more outlets for my pies, and make more money. But at what cost? And those were just one-up business decisions. Franchising was a whole different kettle of fish that took a lot of time to set up, and a lot of input to keep it true to the nature of my business. Finding like-minded folks who would adhere to the Papa D model wouldn't be easy and maintaining it could be frustrating and maybe disappointing.

Then, I found myself thinking about my art. In the confines of my art studio, a lot of unsold canvasses were accumulating, and I found myself back to the classic egocentric place of what is my station in life, a 'pieman', the nickname that I was now being referred to as, or an artist, or worse yet, the driven guy who always wanted to achieve big financial success. I was becoming aware of the time constraints life puts on us all.

But we are all—and I guess I mean most of us—thinking humans, who have an urge to find more meaning in our lives and I was so there in those days.

I had a regular customer who was an executive in an international car-rental business who appeared to be courting me about franchising. One Saturday afternoon, I was playing ball in the yard with my very energetic grandson when he drove in to buy some pies. I put my grandson on hold while we chatted.

"Well," he said, "Have you given much thought to expanding this little gold mine you have here?"

"I have, yes. But I've decided to keep it small, debt-free, eventually sell it, and take up chillin' and paintin'." I glanced over at my grandson who was getting antsy waiting on me and said: "And spending more time with my grandkids, my kids, and my wife."

He nodded towards the boy. "But don't you think you owe it to those grandkids to make a success out of this? It would be your legacy for them."

"Success is relative, man. I have a good living here

and get to spend quality time with my loved ones—it's already a success. Kids don't care about legacies: they just want your time and attention."

"But you told me you just lease this property and there's no telling where you can go with this. Why not get ahead of the situation and fly a bit?"

I laughed. "I've chased the whole 'golden ring' thing a lot in the past but ended up with so much stress and grief, it wasn't worth it."

That conversation helped me immensely with the decision about franchising. June and I had spent many hours researching the concept and agreed it wasn't a direction we wanted to pursue. Having turned away from that connection, I still had to deal with the woman in Powell River I'd left on hold.

Powell River is a beautiful place at the top end of the Sunshine Coast. Getting there required another ferry trip from our peninsula. With an approximate population of fourteen thousand people at that time, it's built on the side of a hill, with ocean views for a lot of its residents, sandy beaches, lakes, and a stable economy. I'd developed a customer base there and was getting large enough orders to justify deliveries, so it was appealing to set up a satellite dealer—but a franchise?

The lady owned a bakery and was under contract with a large grocery store. She wanted to set up a Papa D Meat Pie franchise in her bakery and sell products in the grocery store. We travelled to the area with a large wholesale delivery she'd ordered as a dealer and met with her to discuss the situation. I'd decided to let her down gently. But all that went out the window, when she told us her contract was up for renewal with the store and she'd only just learned they'd decided not to renew. The population base was growing in Powell River and the store was joining the ranks of its big-city counterparts and planned on opening an in-store bakery themselves, no longer needing outside contractors. This knocked her back on her feet because her bakery was suffering the loss of a large contract with them. We could tell she hadn't come to terms emotionally with this devastating news. Still, she decided she wanted a Papa D franchise, but having been through many start-ups of my own, the thought of the stress level she was already dealing with left me cold. We told her we thought the idea should be shelved for now until she'd had time to re-assess her situation.

June and I discussed it on the ferry ride home, and we concluded we would probably not hear back from her—and we didn't. As for our situation? We were making ends meet, enjoying life, and having time for family. So many people on this planet (our only home) spent most of their time on a daily struggle for mere survival; we knew we were very fortunate, and being in good health, we counted our 'blessings', as they say.

I was doing something I loved and something I controlled. I cared about the quality of my product and fussed over every detail like a mother hen. Franchising required tight controls and that would mean constant diligence, which meant inevitable stress. If I was ten years younger, maybe; but the stress wasn't a good thing and something we didn't need to add to the peaceful life we found ourselves living.

As I had learned, sometimes less is more. And so, I put to rest the idea of ever franchising.

Chapter 19

Sometimes Life Is About Risking Everything for a Dream No One Else Can See But You...

—Author unknown

In 2004 the property owner, who lived in Vancouver approached me. He and his wife, and their young son had become friends of ours, so I was saddened when he told me with a heavy heart that their marriage was ending, and he needed to sell the property to settle the divorce. From a business perspective, this could be a blow to my business and personal life. A new owner would be well within their rights to end our tenancy if they so chose, but what then would happen to Papa D's? He offered us an option to purchase the property, but sadly it was at a price we knew we couldn't afford.

Of course, back in 2002 before we even set the whole idea of Papa D's in motion, we had engaged with the landlord about the possibility of him selling the property in the future. It wasn't a frivolous decision on our part to move forward with my business plan. The owner loved this property and never wanted to sell it. He loved living rurally on the coast, but his wife preferred the city. For the sake of job security and economic stability, they'd relocated to the city and settled there—but it was always in the back of his mind that one day they would return to live on the property. There was another house on the front of the acreage they stayed in when they visited the coast. He'd assured us we were secure there with Papa D's for as long as we wanted. For that reason, we'd taken a chance and went ahead with setting up the business and our building.

But life has a way of changing plans. The owner felt terrible, not only for us but for himself. He didn't want to lose the property but had no choice in the settlement but to sell it. So, we signed a new lease with him then and there for three years, believing this would afford us some security with a new owner, who'd have to assure the existing owner that he would honour the existing lease. I knew that in three years, my pensions would kick in and we'd be ready to make some changes anyway. It took a year for the property to sell, and when the new owner took over the property, he honourably but not happily agreed to continue with the two years left on the lease. His attitude was very different from that of the previous owner. Over time, he stated on more than one occasion he believed we should have two different lease arrangements: one for the residence, and another for using his land to run a business. He knew our business was successful and he complained that we should be paying more than we were. It became obvious to us that once our remaining two years on the lease expired, he would hit us hard financially with a new tenancy and business lease. We understood why his discontent was growing: Vancouver real estate prices were hitting our sleepy, rural peninsula, even though we were cut off from the mainland by water and mountains. He knew he was losing money tied into our lease as he was. Money was his motivator and soon we'd have to make some major decisions—but not yet.

Time marched on and I concentrated on my business for the next year. The more I watched the greed of others grow, never satisfied, wanting but not needing more, I reflected on how ego-driven parts of my life had been and I saw the worldview—yes, *Weltbild*. I know now what matters is love, family, and the time we spend with them and not wasting time and energy determining our position in life by the false exterior of our assets, but rather by honestly giving an ear (and hugs) to others. For the first time in my life, I was enjoying small achievements and not seeking approval through unrealistic expectations.

But—I was an artist and had been since I was six years old when the family doctor sent me to after-school art classes for six years. I had deep down thought of myself as pursuing a goal of—what? Greatness? Perfection? Oh, the big bucks? This had been a duel inside me. Oscar Wilde said all art is quite useless. Wilde believed that art need not express anything but itself. He put the value on artistry above anything else and regarded life as a kind of art form, to be lived beautifully. Now, we can all interpret this to fit our psyche. When I read this, I was ready for it. I had become so aware of our human endeavours becoming so transactional, so egocentric, I found myself questioning all forms of art, feeling deep down that any art form was not as critical as human sharing and caring. But if life is 'art', it *is* important—if we put it in perspective and prioritize. Our lives are canvasses, and we can choose how we want to paint them.

So now I was at peace with these feelings and just as the Buddhist Masters teach: When you feel understanding is attained, go back to your village and work.

And that's what I did, loving what I did more than I could've ever imagined: rolling pastry, cooking fillings, baking the pies—and of course, all to music. Music of the soul to me is classical works of all forms and my work in the kitchen was inspired by it. How could my small world inside that kitchen, lost in the music, amidst the smells of baking pies, not take my mind into a place of reflection and enlightenment? This was my meditation.

There were times during my day that would lead me

along the path from the kitchen to our home, entered through my art studio where I'd stop, pick up a watercolour painting or two, and pick up a brush and add a few strokes. Let me tell you about one such journey along the path to my studio, where I was struck with what I can only describe as a thought so complete, it can only be described as a 'Satori' (sudden enlightenment). It became: we're born into this world as we are, with no choice in the matter; as a Tibetan villager, a Russian peasant, a future king, an upper-class New Yorker, an African refugee living in poverty and war. *No* choice, we're just here—so what on earth is prejudice? What right does any of us have to judge, when it comes down to where and how you happened to become a part of this thing called humanity? Being a good human being is a bigger accomplishment than acquiring a position of wealth and all the toys if we are empty inside. Now, this wasn't earth-shattering news to me at this point in my life, but the Satori I experienced in that single moment was—we *must* accept who we are and be at peace. For a po'boy with eight siblings who grew up on the wrong side of the tracks, this was my Satori.

Allow me to digress for a moment with a story from my youth, as a teen growing up in a small Interior town. Those of us who were lucky enough to have a car always gave other kids rides to the beach. One day, the mayor's daughter asked me for a ride, and I obliged. We joined our friends and spent the afternoon at the lake swimming and being the kids that we were. The next day, I was pulled over by the police with a message from the mayor—'stay away from my daughter'. I wasn't to date her or give her rides around town. I can laugh about it now, but as a youngster, this was another reminder of where I'd come from and how I didn't fit into the mayor's world—not because I was a bad kid or ever been in trouble—but because I was born into a family who was poorer than his. Through my Satori, I realized incidents like that one influenced my feelings about myself for a lot of my life.

As mentioned earlier in this story, I didn't have the strong male support and guidance of a dad to guide me during my childhood. My grandfather's wisdom was lost on me in my youth, and it took many years before I felt grateful for his presence in my life and truly appreciated his words One other man had a strong influence on me. He came into my life when I was forty-four years of age when I married my life partner, June. Bob was her father—a principled man, a World War II veteran and amputee, and a hero. He was a man who had no time for self-pity and used humour to face adversity his whole life. A wise man who quietly grokked a situation but only spoke if he deemed it would help. We had many enjoyable conversations over the years and one conversation stands out because it had a profound effect on me. We'd been discussing my past water pump research project and my disappointment in losing funding. Bob had asked me numerous questions about the project, and I'd explained that after I'd lost out on the government grant, I'd attended a meeting with a man in Vancouver known as 'The Godfather of Howe Street', who was involved in the stock exchange and knew all the ins and outs of becoming a public company and finding investors. The Godfather listened to my story and gave me a lesson on working with third-world countries. He advised me on the perils of corrupt governments and greasing the pockets of the right people in a world very foreign to the one I lived in. And even if I could get past the autocracy and my project became a reality and was working for the betterment of the people, there were so many other pitfalls. Like some of the people themselves, so poor, they'd sabotage the water system by stealing some part that they needed to run their personal equipment, and on and on.

My father-in-law weighed all that I'd told him and then he said: "Dennis, you'll never be a billionaire, and I'll tell you why. It's not that you aren't intelligent enough, ambitious enough, or creative enough to become a billionaire because you are. But to be a billionaire you have to work from here." He tapped his fingers on the side of his head. "You? You work from here." He tapped his fingers on his chest over his heart.

Meanwhile, I'd added another side to Papa D's. I'd purchased some antiques like old wringer washers, pedal sewing machines, tin washbasins, baby buggies etc. and set them up for sale on the roofed porch along the side of the old barn.

My customers, especially the tourists, loved walking around the deck with a hand pie in their hands, browsing through a little bit of history. Some bought them for nostalgia, others happily took them home to their gardens to be used as flower containers. Our province has an annual garden contest called 'Communities in Bloom'. The towns compete among their residents, regionally, and provincially for coveted awards and distinction. It's amazing the ingenuity people express when looking for distinctive flowerpots.

So, there I was loving what I was doing, 'playing' in my kitchen, feeling excited when I'd hear the crunch of tires on the long gravel driveway, loving my customers, and truly accepting and loving myself—truly living by the light of my own mind.

Chapter 20

Pie in the Sky and Human Greed...

ONE DAY A STRANGE LITTLE FELLOW ARRIVED AT THE STORE with a request for not a large order of meat pies, but a *very* large order. He was promoting a mountain music festival on Mount Elphinstone and expected thousands of attendees. His group decided my meat pies would be the main fare for the three-day event and assured me facilities would be set up with a generator to provide hot pies. His order was for fifteen hundred pies. *What?* I immediately cautioned him he may want to rethink the quantity as I quickly added up the monetary value of such an order in my head and what it could mean to me. But I'd learned long ago, greed leads to trouble, and not only for me. I wasn't set up to fill an order that size and instinctively I knew his enthusiasm for the festival and the amount of money he expected to make off the catering was clouding his judgement.

A short story from a different time and different business but similar circumstances: Back in 1972, there was a large event in Vancouver called 'Infinity Fair' and the featured act was the Rolling Stones. At that time, I owned a T-shirt company and was the only printer in

Vancouver; my competitors were in Edmonton and Toronto. A promoter came to me with an order for ten thousand various-sized shirts requesting the Stones logo on them. I told him I wasn't authorized by law to print the Stones logo, nor could I fill an order that size in the short time he was suggesting. I further warned him the order seemed far too large for the event.

He was angered by my suggestion his expectation was too optimistic and slapped cash down on the table stating: "Print whatever this will buy, and we'll go from there." We changed the Stones logo to 'Infinity Fair, Stones, 1972' and managed to print a couple of thousand shirts—he sold four hundred. It was a good payback for me but not so good for him. But the fair was a hit, the Vancouver police managed to create a skirmish with a crowd the media labelled a 'riot'—and I had a pissed-off promoter trying to give back hundreds of shirts. I stood up to him and said no. He pulled his best Joe Pesci routine on me and stormed out. Fortunately to this day, I've not heard from him.

So back to my music guy: I went into a mature mode, pushed away my short-term greed thoughts and convinced him to cut back his order to five hundred pies, lesser amounts of blueberry and apple pies, and we were both happy.

Once again, while rolling pastry, this experience sent my thoughts reeling about the human condition and took me back to post-World War II, an era always scary for those of us whose deep fears were stoked by the Cold War of the fifties. Schooled with practice air raid exercises in case of a nuclear war. The Russian thing may not have been part of our everyday conversation as students, but it was ingrained in our psyche, and then came the Korean War which was all too real for some, adding to our constant reminder of the big threat of Communism.

As a race, we humans have a very violent past, and now we had incredible weapons and a motive to use them, not the least of which was the warning from Eisenhower's farewell speech:

Beware of the military-industrial complex. The giant weapons industry fueled by intense greed was very much alive on our little spaceship called Earth.

A quote, I can't recall the writer, pointed out: *We've always been crazy, but were never skilled enough to destroy the world—but now we are.*

So, what does this have to do with baking pies in a little country bakeshop? *Everything!*

I could not stop thinking expansively about our situation and this quote from a book I recently read by Daniel Asa Rose and Rob Anderson summed it up for me: "We are on a microscopic pebble hurtling through space at sixty-seven thousand miles an hour—and people are not curious about the mystery of existence?"

While working at and creating Papa D's comfort foods, I was learning the truth of 'pondering our existence': becoming aware of the human luxury of having time *not* spent on mere survival but finding a place where you have something meaningful to do in providing the means to care for your everyday needs of food, shelter, clothing, transportation, and yes, entertainment. After years of chasing the 'big brass ring' instilled in my upbringing in a small Interior town, their version of success, the American dream of homes, cars, and some degree of fame, I'd found some success but hadn't achieved much satisfaction (thanks, Mick). I'd been looking for fuck you money, thinking more money would make my life easier. Well, folks, it's a myth. Even the rich can be unhappy, never finding satisfaction. Albert Einstein said, 'find a simple and clear image of the world'.

I discovered I was living in a beautiful cedar forest, with fresh air, and the sweet smell of cedar mingled with the succulent smells of baking pies, where I was my own boss, paying my bills.

It comes from within and that's my definition of success.

Chapter 21

When the Toughest Decision is the Right Decision...

It was late 2005 and Papa D's was nearing three and a half years in business. June and I were both collecting small pensions, and she was working part-time at the clinic and part-time with me in the commercial kitchen. We knew we were reaching a crossroad in our lives as two things became apparent. In a year and a half, we'd both be in a position to retire full-time and co-incidentally our lease on the property would expire.

Now the word 'retirement' just wasn't in my vocabulary. Pensions or not, my type-A personality could never succumb to playing golf or sitting at home watching television. I knew to 'survive' retirement, I'd need to have a focus to keep my brain stimulated and functioning. For me, it would be doing my art, or still working part-time at something, as long as it was my own thing, and without the stress of having to earn money to support my well-being. For my wife, it meant having the stress-free time to write novels.

The crux of it was the expiring lease. The landowner had never been in business for himself until he bought this property, and what he saw was a successful business that was making lots of money. He never factored in expenses or labour costs, or the difference between gross and net. He decided we were getting away with something and made it very clear we would be on a yearly lease—one for the business and another for the residence. A yearly lease is never a good thing for a businessman. The average commercial lease in British Columbia is three to five years, five to ten years for larger enterprises. With the Sunshine Coast growing as an extension of West Vancouver with city prices, he was keeping his options open. Properties were being bought up by developers and you could build a lot of townhouses on three acres of land. The writing was on the wall for us; it wasn't a matter of if or maybe but just a simple matter of when.

We were enjoying our business and personal lives and the grandkids were very much a part of our lives. As much as I didn't want to do it and resisted making the final decision, my gut feeling told me we had to sell the business—or at the very least, the building and equipment. If we waited for a surprise visit down the road from the landlord ending our tenancy, we may not be given enough time to deal with selling. Of course, he had to follow the tenancy act, but since he was all about the money, there would be no concessions...this I knew. If we dealt with it now, we could take all the time we needed on our terms without the stress of a set timeline. So, in February 2006, I placed the business up for sale. There were a few enquiries over the next few months, and we rejected a couple of feeble offers.

One couple came to look at the building. The woman wanted to set it up on their property as a home-based business making vegan products. Buying my meat-based business was not on the agenda. It was the building and equipment she was after. Her husband was pleasant enough, but she spent her time wandering from room to room sniffing everything. Finally, she turned to me and divisively said: "But everything smells like *meat*"— she spat the word—"how will I ever get rid of that smell?" I patiently assured her a scrub-down of the premises would solve the problem.

Then, she asked me what I wanted just for the building and equipment, and when I answered she scoffed and said her husband could build her a kitchen for that price (which he couldn't). She haughtily turned to leave without so much as a thank you and walked out the door. I turned to her husband, thanked him for coming while nodding my head after her, and said: "Good luck with that."

One cold, rainy Sunday morning in March, when we had no grandkids visiting, June was in the house working on her first novel, *Winter's Captive*. I was headed to the kitchen to do inventory. I looked up the driveway and saw a fifty-something rain-drenched woman trudging towards me. She had no umbrella, no hood on her wrinkled oversized jacket, and was carrying two large shopping bags stuffed so full things were hanging over the tops. Her long, wet hair clung to her head and rainwater dripped off the tip of her nose. My first thought was she looked like an eccentric, homeless bag lady. I greeted her and asked if I could help her.

"Is this the place that's for sale?" she asked.

"Yes, it is."

"So, it's a meat pie business, eh?"

"Yep," I said, humouring her at this point.

"Could I try one?"

"Sure," I said, leading her into the kitchen. "Do you want it heated?"

"Yes, please. Make it chicken."

While I prepped her pie, she wandered through the building, inspecting everything. Normally, under my license, customers aren't allowed to leave the store and enter the kitchen, and if they wanted to use the bathroom, they were supposed to enter from the deck through the outside door into the storage room for access. But I sensed she had more on her mind than chicken pie and kept an eye on her as she inspected the premises.

She wolfed down her pie from her hand in a few gulps, Aussie style, and said: "Good but needs more salt."

"I leave the salting up to the customer," I said.

"No, I mean the recipe needs more salt."

"Okay," I said, thinking I needed to get this strange woman out of here as soon as possible.

She threw me a curveball. "So, what are you asking?"

I had nothing to lose by playing along and giving her my price, laughing to myself while she wiped her mouth with the wet sleeve of her jacket.

"Can I have another pie—and some salt?"

"Sure," I said. At that moment, I honestly wondered if she even had the money to pay for the pies.

Along came another curveball. "Tell you what, I'm not ready for the building yet, but I'll give you a couple thousand over your asking price, to round it out even—if you give me some time to pay the balance, plus I'll give you a good down payment."

Not sure if she was for real or not, I decided to play it out. "Sounds good so far."

We talked about moving the building to her property on the coast and timeframes.

"My brother is a law professor at Simon Fraser University. If you want to give me a receipt for a deposit cheque to hold it while I get him to draw up the papers, I'll give it to you right now. And then, after I eat my pie, if you don't mind driving me back to the ferry docks, I need a jumpstart. My van has a dead battery."

"Why not," I said to the receipt and the jumpstart, while she wrote me a holding cheque for a few thousand dollars.

On the way to the ferry, she explained to me she

owned a house in Halfmoon Bay (halfway up the peninsula heading north) and often left her van on this side of the water, only to return to a dead battery. She also owned a barista cafe on Commercial Drive, a funky district in East Vancouver, which under the fire regulations wasn't allowed to have a kitchen because it shared a wall with a movie theatre. I kid you not. She could serve coffee and tea but had to import her food products. Hence, she wanted to set up the portable kitchen on her property on the coast and supply her own catered foods. And she wanted to negotiate a separate deal to help her set it up because she'd heard good things about me. The best part was that I could keep the name, Papa D's. We arrived at the van which was full of personal effects, garbage, and stacks of roped LBGTQ magazines, which she said she distributed weekly. This woman was so eccentric and strange (not because of the mags, I'm all for supporting the LBGTQ community), that I was beginning to wonder if she was living in her van and pulling me into her fantasy world.

Chapter 22

The final chapter—or is it???

I can't say I wasn't nervous considering the strangeness of the lady and this weird happening. But—the cheque didn't bounce, we signed the papers, and she gave us a hefty down-payment. Over time, we learned she and her brother were in line to inherit millions from their father who was in his nineties, and she was already receiving a considerable monthly trust fund payment he'd set up for her. She may have been a little off-balance and eccentric, but she was no bag lady and certainly not homeless. (More magic?)

We travelled to Vancouver to visit her cafe next to the movie theatre. It was in a funky location smack in the middle of 'the drive' as it was known; plenty of foot traffic, a cute, cosy spot to be set up for heat 'n' serve and barista-style coffee. I had no doubt it could be a success—eventually. It was full of antiques and nowhere near ready to open. She owned several antique stores in other locations in Vancouver and this busy lady was in no hurry to open the cafe. She was in a constant battle with the City of Vancouver health inspector. I was interested in helping her open and told her I would work with the inspectors. Part of our deal was that back on the coast we could continue to operate Papa D's for one year. She would make three lump-sum payments to us over that time and if she defaulted, we'd keep whatever she'd already paid. This suited her timeline and ours because it would bring us to the end of our lease agreement for the property we were living and working on. With all the other balls she was balancing, the cafe was a pending business she held in the back of her mind to be opened sometime down the road. In the meantime, she was running around buying up real estate on the coast. She needed a manager to keep her focused because she ran helter-skelter wherever her whims took her. That and the fact she was very full-cup as Mac McLaughlin, the Astrologer would say: she was extremely difficult to deal with. I learned to handle her with humour—a very Zen experience.

As a child of privilege, she became a wild child during the hippy years, then taught ESL in Japan for many years. Her saving grace was she had a heart of gold and lived a sharing and caring life. She hired a street person who was down on his luck, gave him a place to live, and he handled any physical work she needed doing on her property or with her businesses. If he needed additional labour, he was instructed to use street people who were skilled enough for the work and needed the money.

As a single woman, her constant companion was Gombi, a full-grown pitbull/Rottweiler cross, which made him larger than the average pitbull. He was rather rambunctious, strong as a horse and he made me more than a little nervous because he was very protective of his mistress. I didn't like him much and usually, he stayed in the van whenever she came by. One day she stopped in on her way back to the coast from the mainland. She tied Gombi to the deck of our residence while we sat inside at the kitchen table chatting. Gombi began to bark, and she yelled at him to stop. A short while later, his barks became higher-pitched and became growl-barks, followed by whimpers. We knew something was wrong and I was the first one out the door to the deck. I stopped short in my tracks as a large bear that could have been Arnold's brother came charging across the yard, heading straight for Gombi, who'd backed away as far as his tether allowed, pulling so hard to free himself he was choking and whimpering in fear. The bear stopped dead at the bottom of the deck stairs when he saw me. It was a make-or-break moment and I grabbed hold of a nine-iron golf club leaning against the railing that I'd found in the brush. Screaming like a banshee, I swung the iron above my head in wide circles. The bear hesitated, stopped, and backed up a few steps. He eyed Gombi, who looked like a cowering, tethered goat; easy prey if he chose. Then, he fixed his eyes on me, appearing to weigh the probability of this wild-eyed, weaponized human hurting him.

I kept up my barrage of shouts and waving my arms, swung the iron fast and hard, and with all the strength I could muster, I threw it at him. It spun through the air just missing his head and hit the tree trunk beside him. It hit hard enough to make a loud thunk and a good-sized piece of bark flew off, causing the bear to turn and fly over the bank behind him. The sound of breaking branches echoed back as he crashed through the brush down to Gibsons Creek and disappeared.

So much for keeping my distance from Gombi, who was smart enough to know I'd saved his bacon. From that day forward, I had to brace myself whenever he came around. He couldn't wait to get out of the van and greet me. His favourite form of affection was jumping up and placing both paws on my shoulders and licking my face. If he decided he liked you, you had a friend for life—and I was his hero. In time, I learned to trust him and liked the old boy.

We added our buyer to our list of Angels; she was

Pieman

definitely a part of the magic of my pie adventure. Meanwhile, as time passed, she made her payments and with only one last payment due, June and I were making plans for the following spring. Being a country boy at heart who'd been raised in the B.C. Interior, I wanted to retire to a small town with lots of open skies, and June agreed. We headed to the village of Clinton, a small hub of about six hundred people consisting of ranchers, mill and forestry workers, home-based businesses, a handful of retailers, and retirees, with a small economic base allowing for affordable real estate. June's sister and her husband had owned property in Clinton for years and recently retired there. It was a perfect location because it placed us halfway between the lower mainland where most of our family lived, and northern Alberta, where our son and his family resided.

What we found in Clinton was a half-acre on a dead-end street with a trout stream running through the back end of the property. A two-bedroom mobile with a two-room addition and a partially closed deck sealed the deal, and we purchased our retirement home. We spent weekends and holidays travelling back and forth from the coast for the next ten months until we could officially retire.

Chapter 23

Wind and Fury...

As we pass through our lives, we all have days and dates that become indelible, never to be forgotten. Thursday, December 14, 2006, and into the following day, was one of those times forever etched in my mind.

It began as any other business day in my commercial kitchen, and I worked through my chores that morning with ease. Early afternoon, I noticed a wind had come up, adding wind chill to an already early wintery day. I'd missed the weather forecast that morning and had no idea of the storm that was brewing off the pacific coastline, about to hit with hurricane-force winds.

The Hanukkah Eve windstorm was a powerful cyclone in the Pacific Northwest region of the US and southern British Columbia, Canada which hit Washington, Oregon, Idaho, Vancouver Island, and Southern British Columbia. The winds hit at 74 mph (119 km/h) and 1.8 million people lost power. When it hit Vancouver, hurricane-force winds ripped through the iconic Stanley Park and levelled 41 hectares of forest. The park lost 10,000 trees, including old-growth conifers that were several centuries old. The structural damage reached 350 million dollars.

Here I was, in a Stanley Park of my own, just north of Vancouver, watching the winds grow stronger,

Pieman

leaves and debris circling in the air, and broken tree branches banging hard against the outer walls of the commercial kitchen, which was wavering back and forth on the cement blocks with only the cemented chains hooked to its metal frame holding it in place. I stepped out on the deck to inspect the premises for any loose objects I should put away and heard a loud crack close by. I turned and looked at the forest behind the house and barn in time to see the top of a cedar tree snap about twenty feet down the trunk, flying through the air, flipping end over end several times before crashing down on the roof of the barn. I marvelled at the ease it travelled through the air considering its size and weight.

I'd had no customers that day and it was eerie to experience all alone what was only the beginning of this massive force of nature. I looked around and realized there was nothing I could do to control the situation or prevent whatever damage it would cause. My eyes fell on my car—I could save my car. It was almost time to drive into town and pick June up at the mall. She was taking the bus from the clinic but getting off at the mall to do some shopping. Maybe by the time we returned, the winds would die down. I left the kitchen and headed to the car. Halfway up the long driveway, the forest ends and the road curves into an open landscape. I stopped at the curve and looked in my rear-view mirror, mesmerized by the swaying motion of the commercial kitchen.

My God! The words of the building inspector rang through my head. *If we ever have hurricane-force winds, the building could break away and leave the flooring secured to the cement blocks. Is that what will happen? Is that what we'll have left, a secured, outdoor dance floor? What about my deal with the buyer?* It had been about seven months since we'd signed the papers. *What kind of tangled financial mess will that create?* Pushing away the troubling thoughts coursing through my mind, I drove on but couldn't stop the pounding of my heart.

I picked June up, who was oblivious of what the south end of the coast was experiencing as it hadn't hit the Sechelt area yet. She was surprised when I filled her in about the tree on the barn roof and the swaying building. Back at the property, we assessed to ensure there was nothing left outside that could be picked up by the circulating gusts of wind and sail through the windows. We also assessed the tree situation and assured ourselves that if any trees beyond the commercial kitchen came down, they were too far away to reach the house. The trees on the embankment at the back end of the property would fall away towards the creek below, or should a sudden gust bring debris in a different direction, it would come down on the open yard area. The only area of concern for us was the forest running along the far side of the house. Our own Stanley Park. There was nothing we could do to protect the house. The car was tucked close to the outside wall of the house away from treed areas. It was as secure as we could make it, so we retired into the house.

We were one of the lucky ones who never lost our power that night, so we watched the evening news and saw the devastation that was happening in Vancouver and the surrounding areas. At one point, we decided to turn in for the night, making a pact that if we heard a tree crack behind the bedroom wall, we'd slide down on either side of the bed to the floor. It was a small room and we each had a wall we could lie against should it be necessary. But as time rolled by, we lay in that bed holding hands, listening to the wind increase and the howling noise become louder, along with the cracking of trees. There was no way we could sleep and since June wasn't working the next day at the clinic, we got up and spent the rest of the night in the living room sipping tea.

Pieman

The front of the house was an open plan and we'd determined the safest place in the house was to lie on the kitchen floor against the front of the fridge and stove that sat side by side, next to the adjacent wall housing a long counter with double metal sinks. It seemed as though a tree came down every few minutes, and we'd learn to gauge how far away it was by the loudness of the crack. We could also guess how many seconds it would take to crash to the ground. Broken branches and debris flew through the air, hitting the deck, windows, and outer walls, adding to the intensity of the night's storm. We could hear the iron chains embedded in the cement blocks straining against the iron-clad underbelly of the commercial kitchen and our ears picked up another treetop landing across the barn roof. We'd never been as scared of Mother Nature as we were that night. At the very least, we knew enough about the distance of the cracking trees to feel assured if one cracked in the forest outside our living room window, we'd have enough time to dive onto the floor in front of the appliances before it hit the house. The windstorm raged on for the remainder of the night and through the early hours of the next morning before it lessened, ending around noon.

We went outside to check on the damage. It was like a war zone out there. Debris, broken tree limbs, and objects like kids' toys that didn't belong to us but were carried in the wind from elsewhere. The house and the car were intact—no damage. The commercial kitchen appeared to have sustained its rock and roll experience and we were grateful for the lockdown chains. Without them, we felt sure the building would have slid off the foundation at some point. The only damage was to the roof of the barn and upon inspection, it looked fixable. Luckily, for us, the freezers we used were near the front of the barn and we could stay away from the damaged area until the owner was able to arrive, remove the trees and secure the roof. Most of the trees that came down were on our neighbour's property and luckily for them, it was at the back of their acreage, away from their house.

Our immediate neighbours had survived with limited damage, all of us personally unscathed, and we emerged having learned to take nothing for granted—especially when we learned eighteen people had lost their lives during that storm, and our thoughts turned to their families.

Chapter 24

Retirement...

The spring of 2007 arrived, and we officially closed down Papa D's and June retired from the clinic. A big life change was coming, and we were excited. Now when you do something this big when you are older, you find you're not as flexible anymore, but we felt we could handle it and we did. We ran a perpetual yard sale as we readied for our move to the interior of British Columbia. Since we'd been travelling back and forth to the interior on holidays and long weekends for the past year, we'd accumulated an almost complete household in our new home; a lot of our existing furniture and duplicate kitchen supplies on the coast weren't coming with us. On the first of May, we set out for Clinton to begin our 'retirement' years with me on full pension and June, at age sixty, on partial early-retirement pensions.

We revelled in our first few years with no schedule or alarm clocks needed to wake us up for work. We found ourselves busy doing renos to our new place, clearing the brush along the fishing creek to give us a clear view from our back deck, and planting flowers. We travelled freely through ranch country with June's sister and her husband, getting to know the back roads. We joined business and community groups in the village of fewer than seven hundred people to learn more about the people who were our new neighbours and their wholesome lifestyle.

We missed our friends back on the coast, but most of all we sadly missed the routine we'd had with our two eldest grandchildren. We'd drive down and bring them back on spring break and during the summer. But over time, we realized it was a transition that would have occurred at some point since they were now teenagers and spending time with their grandparents wasn't half as much fun anymore as hanging with their friends. It was a natural progression that began a little sooner than later. The transition was made easier for us because we had five other younger grandchildren who enjoyed spending time with us in our new home.

Memory Building with the Grandkids

Pieman

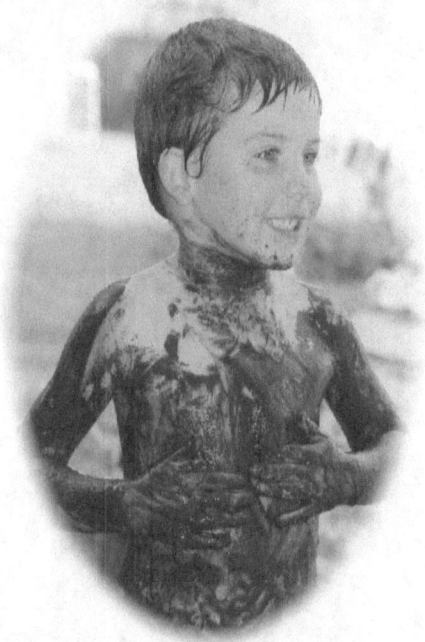

Fun with mud!

Much to her mom's surprise—she never liked to get dirty ntil playing with mud baths!

Pieman

Fishing in the canoe with Papa

Fishing off the bridge to our 'Island'

Clinton's Annual Medieval Fair

Setting up with the neighbour to burn rubber

Pieman

Figures eights in the vacant lot next to our place

More grandkids fishing with Papa D (we have nine)

One of our swimming lakes, Kelly Lake Two
sets of grandkids (cousins)

One of the highlights of our lives was a visit from June's brother and his wife from England. He's always had a fascination with the old west and his favourite movie is *Dancing with Wolves*, which he watches a couple of times a year and never tires of it. We took them on a day-long driving trip through the ranch lands and into the Chilcotin; the semi-arid landscape very much resembles the movie location. They even got to see a bear, a species which is sadly extinct in England in present times. I had a seven-shot 30-30 lever-action Winchester Model 94. Very taken with this western rifle, it made their day to pose (safely) with this classic iconic gun of the west.

As I mentioned in my intro, my business life had revolved around either graphic arts and fine arts or the food business, with a short foray into a scientific research project. To keep busy in this new phase of our life, we'd purchased a vinyl graphics cutter. Living in a six-by-six street downtown with six hundred and fifty people, it certainly wasn't a full-time job. What I enjoyed about it, was being able to incorporate my artistic talent with professional signage. I was a proponent of small is beautiful and was practising living up to the philosophy of living life at a slower pace, enjoying family and friends, and was feeling I'd been able to give up the need for attaining wealth that grips so many others.

The Village of Clinton was on the Historic Gold Rush Trail within the traditional Secwepemc territory in the British Columbia interior, 384 km from Vancouver. The Gold Rush Trail led to Wells/Barkerville in northern BC, 362 km from Clinton. The history of the gold miners can be seen in small-town museums and the architecture still standing along the trail. Some of the signage I worked on allowed me to capitalize on this history and use my artistic skills, making this a fun project.

The signage I painted at the general store drew tourists who loved to stop and read the history, drawing them inside.

Another story from the past—in the spring of 1967, I'd moved my mother to Wells/Barkerville in northern BC with the last four kids of her brood of nine. She'd finally felt in a position to leave my stepfather and raise the last of the kids on her own. Working at the post office, my mother soon knew everyone and developed new friendships in the town that accepted her into the small community. Her ex came to town a few times, trying to worm his way back into her life, and one day some of the men gathered around him and made it clear he wasn't welcome in her life anymore or the town. They suggested he move on, not come back, and he finally left her alone. It was a period where my mother was at her happiest.

Being the eldest, I'd been on my own for many years, but I decided to stay in Wells through the summer of '67 and the winter of '68. I was commissioned by the owner of the Wells Hotel to paint a mural on the back wall of the pub depicting the *Bowron Lake Chain Canoe Circuit*, a famous canoe/portage route that in season draws people from all over the world. He also wanted it to include local animal life.

Back to the future, June and I had lived in Clinton for three years when a friend of mine knocked on the door. He and some friends had been up to Wells and the new hotel owner mentioned he was doing renovations and he wanted to refurbish the mural. They told him they knew the original artist and he lived in Clinton. The owner was excited to find me and asked them to pass on a message to call him. I was blown away the mural had survived for fifty years and called him right away. The deal was a room in the hotel for a week for me and my wife, with substantial payment for the work. June spent time in the room doing final edits to her first novel, *Winter's Captive,* while I spent my time in the pub refurbishing the mural. It was an exciting time for us both and to this day, it's there in its refreshed glory.

Not the greatest pictures to show detail but you get the idea

Chapter 25

Wabi-Sabi...

IN THE SPRING OF 2005, WHILE WE WERE STILL LIVING IN Gibsons, we'd purchased an old wooden boat, a 36' Monk, built in the Allen Shipyards in North Vancouver in 1956. I'd always had a penchant for wooden boats, especially Monks, and the *Black Duck*, as she was called, fit the bill. We never intended on taking her out of the Sechelt inlet to deep seas and enjoyed taking her out to the Provincial Park in Porpoise Bay and anchoring her. She had a deep hull with lots of room in the cabin with a toilet in the bow, a full-sized bed, a small counter with a built-in oven, and even a well-protected small woodstove.

She truly was an ugly duckling, hence the *Black Duck*, but we changed her name to
Wabi-Sabi:

In traditional Japanese aesthetics, Wabi-Sabi is a worldview centred on the acceptance of imperfection. The aesthetic is sometimes described as one of appreciating beauty that is 'imperfect, impermanent, and incomplete' in nature. It is a concept derived from the Buddhist teaching of the three marks of existence, specifically impermanence, suffering and emptiness or absence of self-nature.

She was every bit Wabi-Sabi. She needed a lot of work aesthetically inside and out and would never have been accepted for moorage at a prestigious marina. She was a labour of love and working on her wasn't only satisfying, but relaxing. I repainted her outside and finished the inside with wood slats. *Wabi-Sabi* was our relaxation. There was a swimming platform on the bow and when anchored at the Provincial Park, it provided great access for ocean swimming.

Wabi-Sabi—before we restored her

The happy Captain

On one trip to the provincial park, I misread the tide charts and instead of the tide coming in it was going out. (Yes, I did that.) We were trapped on the sandbar until the tide came back, but *Wabi-Sabi* had stabilizers and we sat perfectly balanced for hours until the tide returned. Despite my stupidity, it was a beautiful day, and June and I relaxed on the boat while watching the grandkids swim and row the inflatable lifeboat, usually tied to the roof of *Wabi-Sabi* for safety. My error turned into a great time for us all.

Grandkids rafting at the Provincial Park

Co-pilot

We intended to use *Wabi-Sabi* as a second home when we retired to the interior. Those were days when moorage costs were affordable, and she became our home away from home when we visited the coast. But as fate would have it, after a couple of winter seasons, she became more of a worry than a joy. When mooring a boat in the northern hemisphere, snow is the biggest enemy for boats and docks alike. Most marinas don't offer snow removal and we lived too far away for winter watch monitoring. We did keep in contact with a couple of live-aboard people at the marina whenever we knew a storm was brewing. Snow adds weight and winds add more rocking. Boats have sunk if not properly cared for. After one fierce snowstorm, we were told by one of the live-aboards that the owners at the marina hadn't shovelled the docks. If the docks don't get enough sun to melt away the snow, in all probability the docks can sink and take a few boats with them. That happened in another marina in Victoria where we had lived in a houseboat. (A story for another time.) Six boats had been sunk along with the dock. Luckily, not when we were living there.

We made a trip down to the coast to make sure *Wabi-Sabi* was secure. Along with the worry, boats can become money pits, and the next summer we decided it was time to sell her and eliminate another winter of stress.

We met a prospective buyer for lunch in Kamloops one Sunday morning. A logger who was working the camps up and down the Sunshine Coast wanted to live on the boat and move it from marina to marina as the jobs moved. He was quite the character, who never ate but ordered beer after beer, instructing the waitress to keep them coming. A deal was struck, a bill of sale signed, and he took wads of hundred dollar bills out of his pocket, waving them in the air while signalling to the waitress to bring him another beer. This caused the other patrons to turn and stare at us—and not for the first time, while he counted the bills out loud, smacking them down on the table one by one. We shook hands with him and skulked out of the restaurant, sure they all thought we'd just completed a drug deal.

Another chapter of our life had closed but we had lots of memories and photos to remind us of our *Wabi-Sabi* days.

Chapter 26
The next chapter...

As much as we loved our retirement time, June and I found ourselves with a lot of downtimes, especially in the winter months when the grandkids were in school and winter roads kept us at home. June was still writing her first novel and had no expectations it would ever be published, and sign work was pretty much dried up in the winter months anyway. Sooo...a part-time position in the Village Municipal Office came up in Administration working with the Chief Administration Officer and it was offered to June. She accepted and went back to work.

About every three months, we'd travel down to the lower mainland to visit family and over to the Sunshine Coast to see the grandkids and friends. More times than not we'd run into old pie customers who begged me to bring pies next time we came down. And relatives of our old customers driving through Clinton to the coast, would stop and ask if I had any meat pies they could buy. With June back to working part-time, we'd often talked about me starting up Papa D's in Clinton. But I knew going in that it would never work on the scale it did down on the coast. First off, we're talking ranchers and small-town residents who grow their veggies and fruits and spent their late summers freezing and canning. These are country folk and the women (and some men) baked from scratch year-round. I also knew highway traffic would be difficult to pull into town and down my dead-end street. Anyway, I didn't want to go back into a full-time business. But as a part-time business where I baked to supply some of my old customers down on the coast when we visited our grandkids would help fill my time, and I truly missed baking.

We decided the back room in the addition, which was currently being used as a storage room could be converted into a small kitchen to serve my purpose. Excited, I drew up plans and took them up to the Health Inspector's offices in 100 Mile House, a forty-five-minute drive north. A visit was scheduled, and the inspector approved converting the room into a kitchen as long as I kept the two doors into the residential areas of the home closed at all times and put a screen door on a roofed open porch where I had a large freezer and space to cool my products. This porch led to the outer back deck.

The feeling of déjà vu set in as I began renos to meet commercial kitchen standards in the new kitchen and the room on the porch, visiting a restaurant supply shop in Kamloops for equipment.

Excitement grew as the day approached for the final approval.

The day the inspector arrived, I'd just finished painting the inside of the outer door to the porch, and I warned her when she entered the paint was still wet. She did her inspection of the kitchen and the outer room with its new screened door and window to the deck, carefully avoiding the wet door. When the job was finished, she stepped back into the kitchen and pulled out a camera. "Just a few photos for the office file," she said. Without thinking, the inspector threw her head and long mass of red curls backwards to get a long shot of one side of the kitchen.

I threw out my arms, yelling, "Careful!" Too late. The back of her head stuck to the wet white paint on the door.

"What's the damage?" she asked, embarrassed.

"Let's just say your red hair is now prematurely white."

In an instant, I became a hairdresser and washed the back of her hair to remove the paint, finishing it off with June's hairdryer. When all was said and done, she turned to me and said:

"Well, who knew when this day started—you'd get your health permit—and I'd get a shampoo, style, and a blow-dry."

And my new kitchen was open for business.

New Cooling Room on Deck

Pieman

Cooling Room—Back in Business

New Kitchen

Utilizing my old signage...and so it begins—again!

Chapter 27

Old beginnings—Bake, Sell, Repeat...

June and I worked out a plan. I contacted all my old customers by phone or email and a great number of them enthusiastically placed orders for my next visit to the southwest. We gathered all their addresses and gave them the date we'd be down to deliver. We planned to start in Gibsons, the first town we'd hit once we got off the ferry, then travel north up the Sunshine Coast to Roberts Creek, Davis Bay, Sechelt, Halfmoon Bay, and Pender Harbour. June had all the addresses on a clipboard in order of delivery. From there, we'd travel to the north end of the coast to catch the second ferry to Powell River (yes, even our Indigenous customers, who'd missed their hamburger pies, renewed their orders). An overnight stay in Powell River was in order, with a return to the south end of the coast to visit family and friends.

I soon got back into routine and filled my large freezer with orders. We had a van in those days and packed it with iced coolers full of frozen meat pies. Our first trip was a success and proved to us that the work we'd put in to set up a new kitchen and a delivery route was going to work. We made enough money off the trip to pay for our product costs and all our travel expenses, and we had a great visit with family and friends. A definite win-win, remembering this was a retirement business to keep me busy and since it wasn't needed to provide an income, it was a lot of fun with minimal stress.

Word began to spread around Clinton that I had a pie shop, and a few residents popped around to see what it was all about. To my surprise, word of mouth spread through the community and locals began stopping in to buy a pie. It didn't take long for me to build some local traffic, just enough to make my new bakery profitable on a very, small scale.

We had a roofed open-sided deck that ran partially down the side of the house near the front, and I decided to close it in and create a store for the locals with a couple of small freezers, my artwork, and small antiques. I did this so I could keep a small number of pies for the locals upfront and separate from my coast orders, and for my customers' convenience so they didn't have to traipse down the driveway, through the gate and around the end of the house to the back deck.

Side deck Renos

Pieman

Inside Renos

All done

The only drawback to this new set-up was when I worked in my commercial kitchen, I couldn't hear customers who were upfront at the store. There wasn't a doorbell on our house, and I devised what I thought was a clever idea. Remember when it was popular to have a singing fish mounted on a board with a button you pushed to play music? The fish's head and tail would move to the beat of the song, appearing to be singing. Yup—I had one of those and loved it. I put it up on the wall with a sign, *Press for service!*

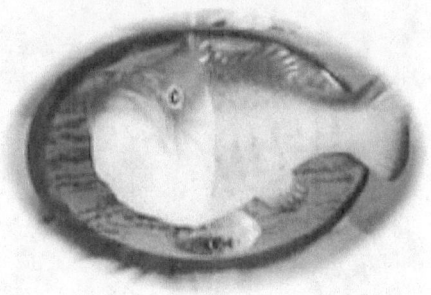

One day while working in the kitchen, the fish started to sing, *Take me to the River!* The next thing I heard was a blood-curdling scream. I ran through the house and out the front door. An elderly woman was sitting on the top step with her hand over her heart. She'd never seen the singing fish before and when the fish began to dance to the music, she almost had a heart attack. Times like these make you realize your sense of humour isn't always appreciated by other people.

About a thirty-five-minute drive south of Clinton, the town of Ashcroft sits in a dust bowl with the railway on one side and the Thompson River running on the other. June and I visited there occasionally to visit my sister and to visit a local coffee shop/bakery for coffee and crullers. One day, to my surprise, I ran into the new owner, an old acquaintance from the Sunshine Coast. He had tables set up inside and outside the shop and asked me if he could put my meat pies on his menu. We worked out an agreement for me to supply him with pies at wholesale prices. Now, I wanted to put up a sign in his shop saying: *We serve Papa D meat pies,* but he said no. He just wanted to add them to his lunch menu. Since it was a part-time business, I wasn't looking to drum up more sales and realized the signage would only be an ego boost. And remembering my search for the meaning of life, I recalled a bumper sticker, *I'm Zen as Fuck!* Sooo—Zen as fuck, I shrugged and said, "No problem."

Fast forward to a day when a Clinton local came into my shop with a story about the owner of the Ashcroft bakery. He'd stopped in for coffee in Ashcroft just as the owner waltzed out of the back kitchen wearing an apron, white flour on his face and hands. He strode from table to table chatting with his patrons and one of them referred to his appearance, "Guess you're busy baking in the back, eh?" To which he replied, "Yup, I'm busy baking meat pies."

To my friend's surprise, I gut-laughed.

"Why are you laughing? He's claiming your pies are his," he said indignantly.

I remembered seeing on the television years ago that Anwar Sadat was assassinated, and I stepped outside to tell my French-Canadian neighbour who was working in his yard. He thought about it a moment, shrugged, and said: "Maybe he need dat."

The memory gave me a chuckle and I turned to my friend and said: "Maybe he need dat."

Yup—Zen as fuck!

Chapter 28

Goodbye to Papa D's...

OVER THE NEXT FEW YEARS, WE MADE THREE TRIPS A YEAR down to the coast to deliver our meat pie orders. June's first novel, *Winter's Captive* was picked up by a publisher and she began book two, *Chasing Georgia*. When she reached sixty-five, she retired to collect her full pensions and dedicated her time to writing. Fast forward to today—little did she know she'd go on to publish seven more books, work on this one with me, and have an idea floating around in her head for book nine. I'm very proud of what she's accomplished.

As we aged, the trips down to the coast weren't fun anymore. We found our day started too early in the morning, and after six hours of driving down to the coast, taking two ferries, and making deliveries all in one day (because we were carrying frozen product), it was becoming too hard for these two seniors who didn't have the stamina we did when we started this crazy business concept. It was time to retire from a business that was too labour-intensive and time-consuming. And so, I decided to shut down Papa D's and dedicate my time to my art—my schedule, always my passion, and a few dollars to be made to keep the old entrepreneur in me satisfied.

Pieman

I sold off the kitchen equipment and the freezers in the store and converted the pie store into a studio.

An eclectic display of BC landscape watercolours, mpressionist, and abstract acrylic canvasses

Always up to trying different creative mediums, a new source of pleasure caught my attention—carving walking sticks, fish bonkers, and shillelaghs. The shillelagh was originally used as a gentleman's weapon in duels and disagreements. Shillelagh fighting is much like sword fighting in that the wielder must skillfully parry and disarm their opponent. So why would people want one in modern times? I certainly had no desire to provide weapons for use in disputes—but for Celtic family pride, historical significance, and for some, fish bonkers for large ocean fish.

The best type of wood for these items is the diamond willow, a hardwood with a twisted shape. When a branch dies and falls off, it leaves an indent in the shape of a diamond in a different shade of colour. Willows grow in low-lying, wet areas and we had plenty of those in the surrounding countryside—in fact, they grew on our property around the creek. Once the bark was peeled, I used a high-gloss stain to protect the wood and to bring out the various colours, accentuating the diamond pattern. When the sticks were finished, a hole was drilled at the top and threaded with a leather strap for a carrying handle; some included wrap-around leather strapping for a solid grip.

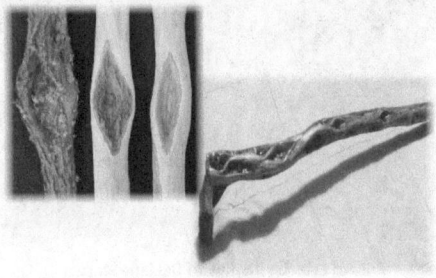

Steps to debarking and the final product

Time passed and when June wasn't writing and I wasn't carving or painting, we travelled the many secondary roads around the B.C. Interior, exploring the landscape and soaking up the history of the area.

Life was good!

Chapter 29

The age card...

As happy as we were living in the interior with its wide-open ranch lands, farmlands, and big skies, a few things happened that sent us on another adventure. As mentioned earlier in this story, we chose Clinton as our retirement place because it put us halfway between family on the coast and family living in Alberta, the next province over. And June's sister was living in Clinton. The four of us spent many hours exploring the land together and we have many fond memories of our travels.

June's sister, Anne, had two daughters living on the coast who had relocated to Vancouver Island. Anne and her husband sold their home in Clinton and moved to the island to be closer to their kids and grandkids. Then, our son took a transfer with the company he worked for and became Island-bound from northern Alberta. I also had a daughter who was living on Vancouver Island. June's mother was in a care home on the coast and was not well; it was a long drive for us to come down regularly to visit her. We took stock of our situation and realized living in a small town with no amenities close by wasn't ideal for ageing seniors without a family support system. Some of the families in Clinton and the surrounding area went back generations and a lot of the people living there had a family support system to help with their ageing family members. The town had a health centre with a rural nurse and a doctor who travelled once a week to our village from Kamloops, a one hour and twenty-minute drive away. Our closest hospital was north in 100 Mile House or south down to Ashcroft. Anything really serious, you went to Kamloops by ambulance or flew by Medi-vac. Missing family and with no support system, we began to question living rurally as we aged. And so, we decided to move to Vancouver Island and be closer to family and June's mom. We put the house up for sale but being in an economically stagnant area, it did not sell fast, and we waited.

Then the unexpected happened that reinforced our decision to sell as being the right one. My doctor arranged for me to have a stress test in the Kamloops hospital because he wasn't happy with the results of some of my tests. Off we went one morning, driving the hour and twenty-minute trip, only to find they were renovating the hospital parking lot and we had to park two blocks away downhill. The two-block uphill walk back to the hospital left me breathless, and since we were early for my appointment, we stopped for a rest at a coffee shop. We took our time climbing the three levels of stairs on the hospital property to reach the entrance doors, with me cursing the whole time about how stupid it was to build a hospital for sick people on a hill. In we went, with me grateful to reach a chair in the waiting room. This was a surprise to me because I'd experienced shortness of breath for the first time a couple of weeks back when riding my bicycle up a short incline in Clinton, which was what prompted me to see my doctor in the first place.

Before my stress test, I was given an ECG, after which a cardiologist was called in and she told me there would be no stress test. She told me the two-block walk uphill was my test. Instead, she told me to walk over to Emergency and check myself in. They were waiting to admit me into the hospital for more testing. A total shock to us both!

The next day, after numerous tests, I was sent by ambulance to the Kelowna Hospital in the Okanagan, a two hour and twenty-minute trip. It was determined that I needed quadruple bypass heart surgery. They sent me to the cardiac ward and marked my chart as a 'widow-maker', meaning they didn't expect I'd survive the surgery. June was told this by the surgeon but not me. They also couldn't understand how I was still walking around and why I hadn't experienced any symptoms months ago. I told them it must be because I was a walker and rode my bike daily. Who knows, but I hadn't experienced anything until those past couple of weeks.

My surgery took longer than usual, and they kept me in an induced coma in ICU so my body could build some strength. When they decided to wake me up, there was my beautiful wife holding my hand, smiling down at me with eyes full of love. I was so grateful to have made it through surgery, my humour kicked in and I used it to cover my emotions.

June said, "Hi, hon."

I stared at her blankly, replying: "Who are you?"

Her face dropped and with eyes full of concern, she looked at the nurse in a panic, who came closer and looked down at me. As drugged as I was, I knew it was a bad joke. I looked at June and gave her a wide smile and winked at her. She almost broke into tears, and told me if I hadn't just had surgery, she'd have smacked me.

I can't say enough about the nurses and doctors at the Kelowna hospital. Their cardiac wing was new and state of the art, one of three in the province at the time. They arranged for June to stay at the BC Cancer building on the hospital grounds. It contained rooms for out-of-town patients from rural areas to stay at when receiving treatments. If rooms were available, spouses of rural patients in the hospital could stay there as well. As luck would have it, June was given access to a room for the duration of the time I was in the hospital.

Three weeks later I was released, and we returned to Clinton. I was looking forward to recuperating on the deck overlooking the trout stream and walking for exercise, replacing my bike with a walker.

I couldn't find a more peaceful setting to heal

Chapter 30

Now? You're kidding, right?

ON MY FIRST DAY HOME, A KNOCK CAME AT THE DOOR AND in came a new acquaintance, a recent newcomer to Clinton. He'd moved to the BC Interior from Alberta and he and his wife bought a ranch north of town. They were part of a family who'd discovered diamonds in the Canadian North-West Territories. He bought up commercial properties in the village and was on the hunt for some residential parcels for members of his family.

His greeting to me was, "Where the hell have you been, man? I've been looking for you for a few weeks and just saw your lights on and figured you were back. I want to buy your place."

You could have knocked me over with a feather and in my weakened state, you could forego the feather. He asked if he could bring his wife around to look the place over and by the end of the day, we had a deal—and to boot, his wife bought six of my walking sticks.

There was one glitch to the whole thing. June tried to negotiate a two-month possession date, but it was a no-go. The buyers needed it in six weeks for his boys to move in as they were arriving on May 1 to help him renovate the ranch house. Six weeks or no deal; he'd look elsewhere. After taking a few years to sell, we didn't want to lose the sale, so we agreed. June's concern was my inability to help. There was a lot to do, and June became a tyrant when it came to me doing any lifting or packing—a definite no-no from the doctors. About all I could do was sort through my art supplies, help her decide what to sell, for what price, and what was garbage. So, while June got to work, I took naps with our two cats, Marbles and Picasso, who never left my side since my return home.

Six weeks isn't very long, and I don't know how June did it with ten years of accumulated 'stuff' to go through. We tried to find a place to live on Vancouver Island, but the economy was booming on the island at that time, and housing wasn't easy to find. June decided we should sell any furniture the new buyer didn't want and start fresh. That way we didn't need a moving van. As far as she was concerned, the easier the move the better, and if we didn't have a home to go to, we'd stay at a motel until we found one. She set up a perpetual garage sale on the property and sold a lot of things online. The last week before we left, June's sister and her husband arrived with a utility trailer and June and John used the trailer to make numerous trips to the garbage dump on the edge of town. Anne and John took most of our belongings back to the island with them. Our son and his wife also came up and loaded their pick-up with more to take back to their home on the island. We decided to follow them back with my paintings and art supplies. Things were falling into place.

Remember the closed-in deck, my former pie shop turned art studio? June took all the leftover knick-knacks, antique washboards, and tea kettles, etc., and the last of the tools we hadn't sold and put them in the now empty studio. If we couldn't sell the last of these items, we'd give them away for free. Down to four days before moving day, I walked over to the local gas station to buy my lotto tickets and ran into the owner of the Clinton Emporium, a well-known antique store/flea market that carries everything western and everything in-between, including the kitchen sink. Being on the highway to Alaska, it was a definite tourist stop. The Emporium is a Mecca for treasure hunters, vintage collectors, and thrift seekers. I mentioned to her that we had a room full of items, some of which she might be interested in.

Clinton Emporium

Twenty minutes later she was wandering around the studio examining the contents. She turned to me and offered me a flat rate—not for a few of the items, but the whole studio. It was more than a fair offer since we planned to give it all away for free anyway. Two hours later her son backed into the driveway and cleared out the room.

All we had left were our clothes, personal effects, and the two cats, all of which would fit nicely in our Dodge Journey. June had done it. She spent the remainder of the days cleaning. After ten years living in what we thought would be our forever home, moving day arrived, and we packed up the aptly named Journey and set off to the island for another adventure

Magic? You bet, I'm a definite believer.

Chapter 31

Becoming Islanders...

THE WEEK BEFORE THE MOVE WHEN WE FOLLOWED OUR SON back to the island, June had checked one more time online for a place to rent. She found a cottage in Ladysmith sitting on a bank overlooking the sea. She called the owner and told him we'd be on the island the next afternoon and would like to arrange a visit. He told her he'd interviewed people all weekend and had one more person booked for the next evening. He interviewed us over the phone and told her if we could get there about 2 pm the next day, he'd show us the cottage.

The next morning, we travelled the six hours to the coast and took the Nanaimo ferry across and made it to his house right at 2 pm. He told us if we wanted it, it was ours, and we were thrilled to know we had a home to move into. He cancelled his 6 pm appointment and we signed the papers right then and there.

The cottage was small, basically a one-bedroom, one bathroom, with an open kitchen/living room, and a tiny room housing a washer and dryer. There was an attached storage shed outside, which was a definite necessity. And a beautiful deck overlooking the ocean. Ladysmith sits on the east side of the island overlooking some of the smaller gulf islands. It wasn't intended to be our forever home, but it was perfect for me to finish my period of recuperation from open-heart surgery, and we moved in with our two cats, two lawn chairs, and an air mattress on the bedroom floor. The next two weeks were spent buying furniture for our new home, while our family delivered the boxes they'd stored for us. We had fun settling in, but it was tiring work, especially so for June, who had to do the lifting and carrying, since the doctors still considered me to be in recovery mode.

We were now eight weeks in from my release date from the Kelowna hospital and we were finally moved, settled in a new home 260 miles away, and June could finally relax. At this point, her body let her know it wasn't happy with the abuse she'd given it for so long. One morning she woke up and couldn't move. Her back was in spasms. We found a clinic and they put her on rest, stretching exercises, and three types of meds: muscle relaxants, anti-inflammatory, and pain relief. She spent the next week lying on the couch stoned, alternating between ice and heat. June was never one who'd suffered from back pain, so it was pure relief when she woke up one morning and it was gone.

I'd been so proud of her strong take-charge attitude and analytical approach to getting the move done and bringing us to the island that I never considered what she was enduring physically. As a man, I can tell you, it left me feeling at my lowest, and the week she was down provided me with an opportunity to give back and take care of her.

Our back deck at the cottage

The beach below the cottage, nicknamed 'Bourgo' Beach by the family

Our resident blue heron lived in a tree above our deck. 'Woodley' was happy to share his home with us (along with his droppings). He'd been living there for twenty years.

We spent the summer enjoying the tranquillity of our cottage, healing, and reconnecting with family living on the island. The grandkids got to spend some quality time with the great-nieces at 'Bourgo' Beach.

Grandkids and great-nieces camping at Bourgo Beach

During my many walks along the beaches, my artist's eyes picked up on the small pieces of wood debris, rocks, and shells weathered over the years and washed up onto the shore. An idea formed in my head and another medium was added to the art projects I called, *'Salish Sea Art'*. And so began a therapeutic journey of gathering and creating sculptures from the bounty given up by the sea. I supplied some gift stores on the island along with my walking sticks, bonkers, and matted watercolours.

Salish Sea Art

Exploring the island and all it has to offer kept us busy and my love of photography was rekindled, which can be attested to by those who are linked to my Facebook page, home to hundreds of pictures I love to post. My photography, depicting the beauty of the part of the world I'm lucky enough to live in, is a passion I love to share with my circle of family and friends online.

June V. Bourgo & Dennis Bourgo

Pieman

A photographer's dream; a trip down the Port Alberni Canal to Barclay Sound on the west side of the island aboard the Frances Barclay

Barclay Sound

We spent three years in the cottage until opportunity brought us to what we hope is our forever home on the south end of the island where our immediate family resides. As our kind-hearted daughter-in-law said, "At least if you both get sick, you are close by for us to bring you some chicken soup."

And they weren't only words. One Thanksgiving Day a couple of years ago, June and I cancelled our plans to join them for dinner because we were both down with nasty flu/colds. A knock came on the door, and we opened it to see our daughter-in-law and granddaughter holding up containers of cooked food for our dinner (and it wasn't chicken soup)—turkey, stuffing, mashed potatoes, carrots, gravy, Brussels sprouts, and even pumpkin pie for dessert. There was enough food for two nights and a turkey sandwich for lunch.

Now, doesn't that just sum it all up about life's journey and what's truly important?

A hot meal from family when you're sick!

I look back on my Papa D years with pride and fond memories. For the most part, life has been good to me, and when I messed up, life gave me another chance. I suppose we all have some regrets when we're reaching our final destination. Understanding that you can't change the past, but you can still change the rest of your journey, says it best.

My final word is this: you can take the baker out of the kitchen, but you can't take the baker out of the man.

Making Pumpkin Pies with Grandchild #6

Kept the Papa D's Sign—a reminder of the magic

I still enjoy making meat pies for family and friends —my journey moves on!

Pieman

The individual has always had to struggle to keep from being overwhelmed by the tribe.
If you try it, you will be lonely often, and sometimes frightened.
But no price is too high to pay for the privilege of owning yourself.

Friedrich Nietzsche

The End

Afterword

Well, that happened!

After a lifetime of struggling to achieve some sense out of this thing called 'life', I came to realize that most of 'reality' is beyond our understanding—from quantum physics to trying to understand consciousness. We are always going to fall short.

However, we must not waiver because in some strange way we'll get beyond 'ego' and achieve some form of peace without wealth, religious bliss, or through 'spiritual borrowing' (drug abuse).

As the song suggests, we may not always get what we want, but if we try, sometimes we might get what we need.

I remember a time in my youth when I was spouting off to my Grampa about the 'state of the world'. He sat in his chair listening as he filled his pipe and tapped it down. He leaned back, sucked on it, and released the poignant sweet smell of smoke while pondering my words.

"Denny," he said, staring into my eyes, "In this world, you need to learn tolerance."

I scoffed inwardly because my definition of tolerance in those days was acceptance, passivity, and subjugation, which meant ignoring and condoning bad deeds.

Afterword

Nothing would ever change or be learned with that philosophy.

As I reflect on that memory, now in my eightieth year and close to the age my Grampa was when he spoke those words, I get it. What he meant was to choose your battles carefully and fight the battles you can win. You can waste a lot of time talking the talk, and spend that time filled with an arrogant rage over things you will never be able to change. That is what Zen as Fuck means to me these days—tolerance.

I can't think of my Grampa without seeing his pipe in my mind's eye. It was his constant companion, even when his memory began to fade and he'd take his daily walks, well into his nineties. He'd wander down the street sucking on his pipe and slip it into one of the big pockets still lit. It seems like yesterday, my Nan, watching him out the window would call out to me and say: "Denny, go put your grandfather out." I'd run down the street to catch up to him, aware that he was oblivious of the smoke billowing out of the burned-out holes of the pocket of his old, ratty sweater.

Time is precious and the short time we get to spend here passes so quickly. If the words written here encourage just one reader to look for the magic and reach for a dream, then I've done my job. Otherwise, I hope you found it to be an entertaining read.

So—did I solve the secret to life during this time of journey in my life? Not on a world scale by any means. But on a personal level?

Absolutely!

About the Author

Dennis Bourgo was born and raised in Vernon, in the North Okanagan area of the British Columbia Interior. An entrepreneur, an artist/photographer, and a writer, he lives on Vancouver Island, off the west coast of B.C., with his wife, June V. Bourgo, a novelist. They have three adult children and nine grandchildren.

His love of painting began at the age of five when the family doctor sent him to afterschool art classes. His works reflect his love of the natural beauty of the province he calls home. His impressionist and abstract style are influenced by his perception of the world around him.

Dennis has published two art books:

Watercolour Thoughts, Musings in Word and Paint, Book 1
Impressions, In Word and Paint, Book 2

June V. Bourgo was born and educated in Montreal, Quebec. June's writing is inspired by the natural beauty of the landscape and the Salish Sea that surrounds her home.

Her writing career began with magazine articles for a single-parenting magazine and writing historical copy. Her love of novel writing grew from there. As an author at Next Chapter Publishing, June has six published novels and a book of short stories to her credit. She writes suspense/mystery stories with strong female protagonists and a touch of magical realism.

Currently, the author is working on a new book, *Beyond Impact*.

* * *

To learn more about June V. Bourgo and discover more Next Chapter authors, visit our website at www.nextchapter.pub.

Other books by this author:

Snap Shots (Life Bites)
The Crossing Trilogy
Magnolia Tree, Book 1
Chameleon Games, Book 2
Storm Dreamer, Book 3

The Georgia Series
Winter's Captive, Book 1
Chasing Georgia, Book 2
Missing Thread, Book 3

Pieman
ISBN: 978-4-82414-874-2
Mass Market

Published by
Next Chapter
2-5-6 SANNO
SANNO BRIDGE
143-0023 Ota-Ku, Tokyo
+818035793528

26th August 2022

www.ingramcontent.com/pod-product-compliance
Lightning Source LLC
LaVergne TN
LVHW032011070526
838202LV00059B/6389